THE
PRAYER-DRIVEN
CHURCH

Cover Design by Mark A. Cole

Library of Congress Cataloging-in-Publication Data

Fulenwider, Ray, 1939–
    The prayer-driven church: releasing God's power to every
    member / Ray Fulenwider.
        p.   cm.
    Includes bibliographical references.
    ISBN 0-89900-864-X (pbk.)
    1. Prayer—Christianity.   I. Title.
BV210.2.F83 2000
248.3'2—dc21

                                        00-021434

I dedicate this book to

thousands of God's praying servants around the world. These men and women faithfully pray for the church to be all that God wants it to be. We need a prayer room in every church with a list of these saints in a Book of Prayer. But they will have something far better as they are listed in the Lamb's Book of Life.

I dedicate this book to

shepherds, ministers, and Christian leaders who pray for God's strength and wisdom to make needed changes for the New Millennium.

I dedicate this book to

Christian Universities, schools of preaching and seminary educators who are teaching their students the power of prayer. What an exciting and important task you have.

I dedicate this book to

the Broadway church in Lubbock, the Richland Hills Church in Ft. Worth and the Central church in Amarillo for teaching me so much about prayer.

I dedicate this book to

the Spring Woodlands Church in Houston for your great expansion dreams and for your desire to always be a "prayer-driven church."

I dedicate this book to

Ron Freeman and Bill Johnson, two shepherds at Central, for their example of prayer in coping with serious illness.

I dedicate this book to

every mate, parent and child who have poured their hearts out to God in prayer.

I dedicate this book to

thousands around the world who pray for me. I would never have made it through the tough times without this.

I dedicate this book to

every Bible school teacher who has taught each student to pray.

I dedicate this book to

Jana and Jeana for typing much of this manuscript and to Joel for teaching me some computer skills.

I dedicate this book to

Deana, Jeana and Jana for teaching me the tremendous power of prayer.

I dedicate this book to

my wife Ann, who spends many hours in prayer for me daily.

I dedicate this book to

my mother, Cleo, who taught me how to pray and to every parent who has taught their children to pray.

TABLE OF CONTENTS

Preface

"[We] will give our attention to prayer and the ministry of the word." Acts 6:4. I never intended to write another book after *The Servant-Driven Church.* Writing is difficult for me, and the response to the book from all over the country has been overwhelming. The e-mails, calls, cards, faxes, letters, book reviews and speaking opportunities have been the most humbling experience of my life. It took ten years to write *The Servant-Driven Church,* and I just celebrated my 60th birthday. Since I have been preaching since the age of 12, I should have been content to thank God and readers for their tremendous encouragement to this lowly servant.

But in the spring of 1999, I awakened one night from a dream about "The Prayer-Driven Church." Acts 2:17 states that "your young men will see visions, your old men will dream dreams." I told my wife that I believed God wanted me to write a book on this topic. I didn't have anything but a title, but I felt "called by God" to write this book. I know this statement probably bothers some people, but I can't explain it any other way.

During the next month, I committed myself to prayer and study on this topic. I didn't want this to be Ray's message — I wanted it to be God's message for the third millennium. I still lacked faith, but I called College Press to see if they would be interested in this topic. I thought they would turn me down because I didn't have a manuscript — all I had was a DREAM! To my surprise, they said: GO FOR IT!!

Servant Hands and Praying Hands

There are servant hands that help and comfort,
Hands that plan and teach,
Hands that touch and hands that strive
For a goal just out of reach,
Hands that serve and hands that give,
Hands that work day by day,
Friendly hands and loving hands,
That serve Christ's church today.
But praying hands are dearest
In the sight of God above,
For in their sweet and earnest clasp
Are reverence and love.
Satan runs from praying hands;
The church is in God's care.
We cannot sin against our Father's love
When hands are clasped in prayer.
— Ray Fulenwider

Introduction

There is nothing as important as prayer for the third millennium! It drives me to my knees when I read that David said, "I am a man of prayer" (Ps. 109:4). What a great statement for a funeral or tombstone. I have never met a man or woman who said they prayed too much. I certainly felt inadequate to write this book, but the more I prayed, the more God answered!! "If you believe, you will receive whatever you ask for in prayer" (Matt. 21:22). God promises the power — why don't we claim the promise?! What would happen if all the churches were prayer-driven churches following Scriptures like these?!

"My house will be called a house of prayer" (Matt. 21:13).

"After they prayed, the place where they were meeting was shaken. And they were all filled with the Holy spirit and spoke the word of God boldly" (Acts 4:31).

"I do not run like a man running aimlessly" (1 Cor. 9:26).

"Let us run with perseverance the race marked out for us. Let us fix our eyes on Jesus, the author and perfecter of our faith" (Heb. 12:1-2).

"I have finished the race, I have kept the faith. Now there is in store for me the crown of righteousness" (2 Tim. 4:7-8).

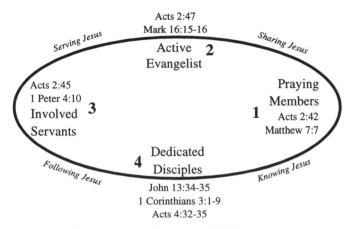

Acts 2:47
Mark 16:15-16

Serving Jesus

Active 2
Evangelist

Sharing Jesus

Acts 2:45
1 Peter 4:10
Involved 3
Servants

Praying
Members
1   Acts 2:42
Matthew 7:7

Dedicated
4   Disciples

Following Jesus

Knowing Jesus

John 13:34-35
1 Corinthians 3:1-9
Acts 4:32-35

Four Quarters in a One-Mile Racetrack

Jesus *PAID* it all for me.

> *P* raying members
> *A* ctive evangelist
> *I* nvolved servants
> *D* edicated disciples

All to Him I owe!

Since this one-mile racetrack "pattern" serves as an outline for the entire book, let me explain the four major points. The New Testament has much to say about "The Christian Race" so this makes a great biblical example. We don't run aimlessly as we have goals and priorities to follow (1 Cor. 9:26). We fix our eyes on Jesus as we run (Heb. 12:1-2).

The biggest religious movement in the world today is "WWJD" (What would Jesus do?). Relating that motto to our study, we will follow Jesus around the racetrack. For the first quarter of the race, we want to concentrate on *knowing* Jesus. We want to let him speak to us through the Bible so we can know more about him. We want to talk daily in prayer to this person we love. We first want to develop **Praying Members** in the

Ponder this:

Why is developing *praying* members the first priority?

We first want to develop
Praying Members
in the church.

church. They need to know who we are, what we believe, and what our Mission, Vision, and Values are — but more than anything else we need to develop praying members. Jesus said in Matthew 7:7 "Ask and it will be given to you." Toward the end of his earthly ministry, Jesus said, "My house will be called a house of prayer" (Matt. 21:13).

In the early church, the new members devoted themselves to prayer (Acts 2:42). "After they prayed, the place where they were meeting was shaken. And they were all filled with the Holy Spirit and spoke the word of God boldly" (Acts 4:31).

Do you want visitors and conversions?—PRAY!

Do you want members to share Jesus?—PRAY!

Do you want more people to serve Jesus?—PRAY!

Do you want better spiritual leaders?—PRAY!

Do you want more people involved in ministry?—PRAY!

Do you want more dedicated disciples of Jesus?—PRAY!

I have never seen a modern church growth pattern (or paradigm) begin with prayer as the first step. But I am overwhelmed when I read the Bible to learn they first prayed before every major undertaking. Examples like Jesus praying before he chose his disciples, Jesus praying in the garden before he went to the cross for us, and prayer in the Upper Room before the Pentecost Revival "jump out" of the Scriptures.

The second quarter mile is a radical departure from most patterns, but it is a very biblical pattern. The new converts became **Active Evangelists** who went out and *shared* Jesus with their friends. Study after study shows that new converts can be the best soul winners. They have just discovered the "pearl of great price," and their friends are still in the world. The early church grew rapidly because of this principle and "the Lord added to their number daily those who were being saved" (Acts 2:47).

> Study after study shows that new converts can be the best soul winners.

For your consideration: What is it about new converts that makes them such good soul winners?

13

They may not have known a lot of doctrine, but they did know enough to tell people how to be saved. Let's not make evangelism too complicated for the third millennium. Each person can share "his story" of why he became a Christian. There is also some alarming research that shows that the longer we are Christians, the fewer people we bring to Jesus Christ!

The third quarter of the race stresses *serving* Jesus. We need to help members discover the spiritual gifts that God has given them to serve others (1 Pet. 4:10). The early church served in taking care of the needs of others (Acts 2:45). We need to develop a great army of **Involved Servants**.

The goal of the fourth quarter of the race is to produce **Dedicated Disciples** who are *following* Jesus. These members become spiritually mature feasting on the meat instead of the milk of the word. They are unselfish servants and are called God's fellow workers (1 Cor. 3:1-9). All people know they are disciples of Jesus because of the great love they have for one another (John 13:34-35). The goal is to finish the race with a mature faith and receive a crown of righteousness (2 Tim. 4:7-8).

The Christian, throughout the entire race, has prayer-driven power from God because "in him we live and move and have our being" (Acts 17:28).

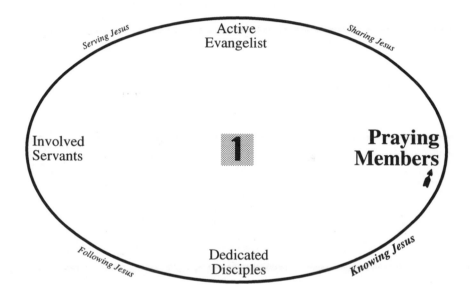

The Power of Prayer

The Central Church of Christ was in serious trouble in 1991. They had been devastated by a financial depression and were about to close the doors of the church building. Building payments were $22,000 a week and contributions were $21,000 a week. It doesn't take a calculator to realize that this was a crisis of gigantic proportions. Central had lost 800 members. The church was facing major staff problems and many staff members had left. Even the great servant pulpit minister Dick Marcear had resigned and was moving to Oklahoma. God had used Dick to build Central from a 500 member church to a 2,000 member church before the financial disaster came. Some elders were declaring bankruptcy, and another elder was involved in a terrible divorce. The 6-million-dollar debt looked like "Goliath" and things looked hopeless.

It was at this time while I was living in the Nashville, Tennessee, area that I got a call from Bill Johnson. Bill was an elder at Central. Someone was applying for a job at Central, and I had been used for a reference. During this telephone conversation, I made the strangest statement. I said, "Bill, I might be interested in coming to Central!" He said, "Could you come for an interview today?" I said, "I guess I can." I called my wife and told her I was going to Amarillo. She asked why, and I said I guess it was to look for a job. There was a long silence on the other end of the phone, and I assumed she had passed out! After a few moments, she asked when I would be back, and I told her I would be back the next day.

When I arrived in Amarillo, I learned more about the impossible situation. But I also learned something of much greater importance. The elders had committed the PROBLEM TO GOD. They knew they could not handle it, but they knew GOD COULD. They began every elders meeting on their KNEES IN PRAYER! They delegated the financial problem out to a small group of men — and they resolved to get back to their task of being shepherds.

Why worry when you can pray?

I attended the most unusual meeting I have ever attended. The elders got on their knees and PRAYED FOR A SOLID HOUR! That was the INTERVIEW.

I then met with the education ministry. Following this, one of the elders gave me his car keys, and told me to visit my ill dad two hours away in Childress! A few weeks later, I was ON THE STAFF AT CENTRAL! And GOD DID MIRACLE AFTER MIRACLE AS HE ANSWERED OUR PRAYERS.

Here is what God did in answer to our prayers:

1. We asked for a special contribution of $150,000 to keep the doors open, and God supplied!
2. We got the building refinanced with lower interest rates and weekly payments dropped form $22,000 to $10,250 a week!
3. Dick Marcear decided to stay at Central!
4. There was thunderous applause as Dick and his wife Lou Nell stood on the stage and the elders announced they were staying!
5. Central started growing again!
6. Staff has grown to 13 ministers, 2 full-time elders, and 6 full-time secretaries!
7. Contributions have grown from $21,000 to $34,000 a week!
8. Mission contributions have grown by $150,000!

If there is any one thing I would stress more in my past years of ministry, it would be PRAYER. If there is any one message I would like to emphasize as we approach the third millennium, it is the POWER GOD PROVIDES WHEN WE PRAY.

I highly recommend John Maxwell's book, "Partners in Prayer." John says that the Prayer Partners ministry was the greatest thing that had ever happened to a church where he had worked. Max Lucado writes in the foreword of the book that nothing had helped "his church" like this Prayer Partner Ministry.

I've conducted over 360 leadership retreats with the finest men and women in the world. These people have many worries and concerns. Many are frustrated and about to give up. There are church problems, marital problems, family problems, health problems, decision problems, shepherding problems, leadership problems, personal problems — we must PRAY for GOD'S WISDOM, which He promises, and discover what God can do when we PRAY! In Acts 16 we read that the troubled Paul and Silas, in jail with numerous problems, were praying instead of complaining and shouting instead of pouting! And, God heard their PRAYERS and ANSWERED!

> The troubled Paul and Silas were praying instead of complaining.

Points to ponder: Why don't we pray more? What happens when we don't?

What happens when we don't pray?

1. We don't get what God wants us to have.
   "You do not have, because you do not ask God" (Jas. 4:2).
2. We hurt God's work.
   "If my people, who are called by my name, will humble themselves and PRAY and seek my face and turn from their wicked ways, then will I hear from heaven and will forgive their sin and will heal their land" (2 Chr. 7:14).
3. It shows our lack of faith in God.
   "Without faith it is impossible to please God" (Heb. 11:6).
4. It shows our laziness (prayer is hard work).

19

"[Jesus] prayed more earnestly, and his sweat was like drops of blood falling to the ground" (Luke 22:44).
5. We have less important priorities.
"[We] will give attention to prayer" (Acts 6:4).

Claim the promises in these power verses:
1. "Ask and it will be given to you" (Matt. 7:7).
2. "For everyone who asks receives" (Matt. 7:8).
3. "Ask and you will receive" (John 16:24).
4. "How much more will your Father in heaven give good gifts to those who ask him!" (Matt. 7:11).
5. "If you believe, you will receive whatever you ask for in prayer" (Matt. 21:22).
6. "You may ask me for anything in my name, and I will do it" (John 14:14).

Prayer is the key to heaven, but faith unlocks the door.

Consider: With verses like this, I'm now not so
How do you surprised when I hear the following stories which my
explain God's human finite wisdom cannot explain — but to God be
answers? the glory.

1. A small girl drowns in a hot tub and electrical stimulation was used twice to restart her heart. The doctors see no hope. But she is alive and healthy today, and medical doctors say prayer saved her.
2. An 80-year-old man is about to die, and the family calls for the elders of the church to pray and anoint him with oil. The man lives and goes home from the hospital.
3. Over 100 people gather every Tuesday night in a home to pray for one another. They give incredible testimonies about the power of God.
4. A man obeys the gospel after 10 years of marriage. The wife is not surprised because she has been praying for him every day for 10 years.
5. A young man is a near alcoholic and spends most of his time in the bars. He can't hold a job and crashes

two cars. Through e-mail, letters, and phone calls hundreds of people pray daily for this young man. His life straightens out.

6. A husband and wife are having terrible problems. It looks like a divorce is imminent. But they commit their time to daily prayer and call for daily prayer from their new prayer partners. The marriage is saved.

7. The church is about to split. All the alternatives look bad. The elders spend two hours on their knees in prayer. God provides a miracle!

The Acts of Prayer

A good way for us to more deeply appreciate the power of prayer in the early church is to go through the book of Acts with a highlighter and highlight each passage that deals with prayer. The book of Acts will come alive with the power of prayer when we look at verses like:

Acts 1:14 — "All joined together constantly in **prayer**" in the upper room.

> Go through the book of Acts and highlight each passage that deals with prayer.

Acts 1:24 — They **prayed**: before selecting a new apostle.

Acts 2:42 — The new believers "devoted themselves . . . to **prayer**."

Acts 3:1 — " Peter and John were going up to the temple at the time of **prayer** — at three in the afternoon."

Acts 4:24 — When Peter and John were released from confinement, "they raised their voices together in **prayer** to God."

Acts 4:31 — "After they **prayed**, the place where they were meeting was shaken."

Acts 6:4 — "We . . . will give our attention to **prayer**."

Acts 7:59-60 — "Stephen **prayed**, . . . 'Lord, do not hold this sin against them.'"

Acts 8:22 — Peter to Simon: "Repent of this wickedness and **pray** to the Lord."

Discuss:
How much
was prayer
emphasized
in the book
of Acts?

Acts 8:24 — "Then Simon answered, '**Pray** to the Lord for me.'"

Acts 9:11— "Ask for a man from Tarsus named Saul, for he is **praying**."

Acts 9:40 — "Peter . . . got down on his knees and **prayed**."

Acts 10:2 — "[Cornelius] **prayed** to God regularly."

Acts 10:4 — "Your **prayers** and gifts to the poor have come up as a memorial offering."

Acts 10:9 — "Peter went up on the roof to **pray**."

Acts 10:31 — "Cornelius, God has heard your **prayer** and remembered your gifts to the poor."

Acts 11:5 — "[Peter] was in the city of Joppa **praying**."

Acts 12:5 — "Peter was kept in prison, but the church was earnestly **praying** to God for him."

Without prayer you can't please God.

Acts 12:12 — "[Peter] went to the house of Mary . . . where many people had gathered and were **praying**."

Acts 13:3 — "After they had fasted and **prayed**, they placed their hands on them and sent [Paul and Barnabas on the mission trip]."

Acts 14:23 — "Paul and Barnabas appointed elders for them in each church and, with **prayer** and fasting, committed them to the Lord, in whom they had put their trust."

Acts 16:13 — "We expected to find a place of **prayer**. We sat down and began to speak to the women who had gathered there."

Acts 16:16 — "Once when we were going to the place of **prayer**, we were met by a slave girl."

Acts 16:25 — "About midnight Paul and Silas were **praying** and singing hymns to God, and the other prisoners were listening to them."

Acts 20:36 — "[Paul] knelt down with all of them and **prayed**."

Acts 22:17 — "When I returned to Jerusalem and was **praying** at the temple, I fell into a trance."

Acts 26:29 — "Paul replied, 'Short time or long—I **pray** God that not only you but all who are listening to me today may become what I am, except for these chains.'"

Acts 27:35 — ""[Paul] **gave thanks to God** in front of them all."

Acts 28:8 — "Paul went in to see him and, after **prayer**, placed his hands on him and healed him."

2 Prayer in the Early Church

"One day Jesus was praying in a certain place. When he finished, one of his disciples said to him, 'Lord, teach us to pray'" (Luke 11:1). Jesus then taught them seven principles of prayer:

1. Praise the Father's name.
2. Pray for the Kingdom.
3. Pray for his will to be done.
4. Ask him to provide our daily bread — sustenance.
5. Forgive our sins — forgiveness.
6. Lead us not into temptation — guidance.
7. Deliver us from evil — protection.

Consider carefully: If Jesus visited us for a week, what lessons would He give us about prayer?

Jesus was the world's greatest preacher and teacher, but no one ever asked him to teach them to preach. He was the world's greatest miracle worker, but no one asked him to teach them to do miracles. But when they heard him praying, one of his disciples said: "LORD, TEACH US TO PRAY." His powerful example and teaching on prayer had a profound effect on the early church. In the last chapter, we traced the emphasis of prayer throughout the book of Acts and that emphasis seemed to continue for many years after the Bible account closes.

The Jewish synagogue had a great influence on the early church. Even though what we know of the practices of Jewish synagogues mostly comes from later centuries, some of these later practices are certainly carryovers from the time when the early church was being established and influenced by its Jewish roots. Synagogues were noted for being houses of instruction, but prayer was also a vital part of the service. At least ten people had to be present for the regular worship. Key people in the worship service included:

1. The elders — acted as a Committee of Management of the affairs of the synagogue.
2. The ruler — was chosen from among the elders. He controlled the services, decided who was to read from the Law and the Prophets, as well as who was to preach. He was also responsible for the discussions.
3. The servant — kept the building clean and was responsible for the physical arrangements. He taught the children and was usually responsible for discipline.
4. The delegate — was chosen for each meeting by the ruler and he conducted the prayers. He usually read the prayers as well as passages from the Law and the Prophets. He had to be a man of extremely high character.
5. The interpreter — translated into the common language of the people (Aramaic) the passages of the Law and the Prophets which were read in Hebrew.
6. The almoners — at each service collected alms for the poor and also distributed the money to those in need.

The order of the service was also very interesting:

1. The congregation recited the "shema" together. It was a confession of God's unity taken from Deuteronomy 6:4-9; 11:13-21; Numbers 15:37-41. Blessings were expressed before and after the recitation.
2. Prayer Time: The most important prayers were "Eighteen Eulogies" which were rotated in their reading. The prayers read by the delegate were always followed by a hearty "Amen" from the congregation.

> The prayers read by the delegate were always followed by a hearty "Amen" from the congregation.

3. Reading of the Law and the Prophets: This was organized so that the Pentateuch (first five books of

the Old Testament) was read through in order every three years.

4. The Sermon followed the reading. It originally was an exposition of the law, but it became more devotional in nature as the years passed.

5. The Benediction prayer followed the service and the congregation answered "Amen" to end the service.

Prayer not only was important in early services; it occupied an important place in the daily life of Christians. The Didache stated that believers should pray three times a day. The Lord's Prayer was used as a model to follow, and daily prayer times for the Christian became 9:00 a.m., 12:00 noon and 3:00 p.m. There was also a private morning prayer when the Christian awakened and private evening prayer before he went to sleep at night. Christians also prayed before and after their meals! There were also community gatherings for prayer and instruction. Contrast this with surveys today that show the average Christian prays less than 30 minutes per week including services!

> Prayer not only was important in early *services*; it occupied an important place in the *daily* life of Christians.

The **ACTS** acrostic is a good outline for the model of balanced prayer in the early church:

> **A**doration — We offer adoration and praise to God.
>
> **C**onfession — We confess our faith and we confess our sin.
>
> **T**hanksgiving — We thank God specifically and generally for everything He has done for us.
>
> **S**upplication — We request various things from God which we need.

"Amen" became the common way to conclude prayers. It means "may it be so," or "it is true." But other phrases were also used in prayers or at the conclusion of prayers. "Hallelujah" was one of these expressions, and it means "Praise the Lord." "Hosanna" was a word often used, and it meant "save now." "Maranatha" was another common expression which meant "Our Lord, Come."

Posture and physical expression in prayer were varied in the early church. Some bowed and knelt. Others lifted up their hands and heads and looked up. Some placed their heads on the ground and others stood and beat their chests.

Think about it:
What is your response to the different prayer postures described?

Looking upward to God with hands extended upward and palms open was a very common prayer posture. It symbolized gratitude to God; the hands were open in expectation of the blessings that God would give. It was almost as if I am expecting God to throw many blessings back to me, and I'm symbolically catching them with my hands. It portrayed catching a "shower of blessings" from God.

With prayer you can move mountains.

This same posture was often followed by the folding of the arms across the breast. This was an expression meaning: "Thank you God with all my heart."

Pictures in the catacombs of people standing and praying show some holding their hands up bent at the elbows forming a W. This was supposed to symbolize that they were making a prayer request to God. It was also used at funerals to symbolize a deceased person's soul ascending into heaven.

Another early prayer position was fully extending the arms straight out so that the torso and arms form a cross. After a few minutes, the arms become very tired and painful. This was referred to as the "vigil of the cross," and was used by people to "get in touch with what Jesus did for you."

Beating the breast in early Christian prayers meant "I have sinned" and "I will learn well" from my mistakes.

Most of us were probably taught to bow our heads and clasp our hands when we pray. The bowed head has always been a symbol of humility. But the earliest evidence of a prayer with the palms and fingers joined in a kind of steeple was not until the ninth century. It goes back to the practice of shackling a prisoner's hands with a rope. Joined hands came to symbol- ize a man's submission to his master. In Roman times, a captured soldier could immediately save his life by bowing his head with the hands clasped in a prayer pose. It meant "I surrender all" and "I'm your humble servant."

Prayer is cooperating with God in changing me.

Most people think that the "sign of the cross" — a touching of the forehead, heart, left, then right, shoulders with the first three fingers of the right hand — is a Catholic-only sign of prayer. But its beginning actually goes back to the early Christian church. When the church suffered wide-scale persecution, believers used the "sign of the cross" as a secret code for quick identification of one another. It was a rapid stroking of the forehead, and sometimes included the breast and shoulders. It silently communicated, "I am one of you." It was used for identification in much the same way as the sign of the fish.

The three fingers — thumb, index, and middle finger — symbolized the Three Persons of the Trinity: Father, Son and Holy Spirit. The two fingers tucked toward the palm signified the divine and human nature of Christ. The cross was a sign of God's grace and love.

Later, the "sign of the cross" became such a predominantly Roman Catholic sign, Protestants totally shunned it following the Reformation

I wish we could restore the priority, family spirit, enthusiasm, gratitude, prayer time, and closeness that the Lord's Supper had in the early church. They actually called it Eucharist which meant "thank you." As the family of God, they wanted to say thank you to a loving Father for all he had done for them. Since the gospel was taught every day in the early church, God added souls to the church daily. But Sunday during communion was the official welcome for these new converts. They were greeted with a "Holy Kiss," welcomed to the church family, prayed for as people thanked God for their conversion, and served communion first as this became an incredible "eucharist" or "thank you" service to God. All the people would repeat "in Jesus' name" and "Amen" following the prayer.

> I wish we could restore the priority, family spirit, enthusiasm, gratitude, prayer time, and closeness that the Lord's Supper had in the early church.

Ponder this: From the way you treat these events, how would a stranger understand your view of the Lord's Table and the welcoming of new members?

"In Jesus' name" meant "I believe in him, I respect him, and I will submit to him. I will be faithful to his mission and submit to his will for my life." An "Amen" affirmation meant "this is true" — "so be it." Wow! What a welcome class this must have been! What a change this would make in the Lord's Supper and new members for the Third Millennium.

29

3 The Ministry of Prayer

Prayer can do what nothing else on the face of this earth can do! I experienced this firsthand when Mother died with cancer at the age of 48. She had been in the hospital in Childress, Texas, for 21 consecutive days and her body was racked with pain. As an only child, I struggled going through this ordeal. My wife, Ann, was an angel of compassion as she took care of Mother. But Mom died on the 21st morning at the hospital. As she was drawing her last breath, Eldon Sanders walked into the room. He was the minister of the Kirkland Church of Christ and was one of the greatest spiritu-al influences of my life. He had bap-tized Dad, Mom, and me. He had taught me about "church work" as we "chopped cot-ton" and "pulled bolls" to-gether on his farm. He was known as a great man of prayer, and his favorite book of the Bible was the book of Psalms. He practiced what he preached! He grabbed Dad's and my hands as we held on to Mom's hands. He started quoting the 23rd Psalm, and then we had a season of prayer. I experi-enced a time of peace, faith resurgence, and spiritual strength like I had never experienced before. I marveled at the power of prayer.

Prayer is claiming God's promises and applying them to my particular problems.

I returned to the Broadway Church of Christ in Lubbock after the funeral with the determination to start a 24-hour prayer ministry. There were many obsta-cles which had to be overcome:

1. What room would we use for prayer?
2. What kind of physical arrangements would we have in the room?
3. How would we provide security for people since the building was not located in the safest part of town?
4. How could we get people to come and pray?
5. Should entire families come together?
6. How could we remind people to come hour after hour?
7. How could we prepare a prayer notebook for people to follow?
8. Who would prepare the notebook?
9. How would we handle prayer request calls?
10. How would we get people to come at 1:00 a.m., 2:00 a.m., 3:00 a.m., 4:00 a.m., 5:00 a.m., holidays, etc.?
11. What would you do if you were unable to come for your prayer time?
12. What would it cost?

These were tough questions. But, the prayer-driven church sees obstacles as opportunities for God to work "miracles." And He did!!

We finally found a small room in the education building which was not being used. It had virtually been a junk storage room for many years.

> The prayer-driven church sees obstacles as opportunities for God to work "miracles."

God did wonders out of that junk room! It had an outside door that automatically locked when it was closed. Now, all we had to do was make 144 keys for the families that God would provide for us. We went to the benevolent room at church and found a small table, two chairs, a couch, a lamp and some throw rugs.

Police said they would patrol the area and provide security for us. They were pretty enthused about a prayer ministry.

We had four Sunday morning lessons on prayer

31

What do
you think:
Is it possible to
develop a
prayer room
ministry in your
congregation?

with sign-up sheets all around the auditorium. At the end of the fourth Sunday, we had all 144 hours filled! Texas Tech University students had taken those early morning hours.

My education secretary agreed to prepare the prayer notebook. With the exception of new prayer requests, the notebook was only changed once a week. We had a different emphasis each week. It might be families, children, teens, church leaders, teachers, deacons, ministers, elders, community leaders, missionaries, national prayer concerns, the sick, new babies, etc. Prayer requests were also added to the notebook each week. Each praying family could also add requests.

We added a phone to the prayer room, and the first thing each person did when they entered the prayer room was to call the person responsible for the next hour. This reminder telephone call really worked. We also received prayer requests on the phone from the church and the community.

We kept the instructions as simple as possible for the prayer leaders.

1. If you could not fulfill your prayer hour, you were responsible for getting someone to take your place.
2. As soon as you arrived, be sure to call the person responsible for the next hour.
3. Begin with the prayer notebook for your prayer time.
4. Bring your entire family or you could pray alone.
5. Be sure the door was locked each time.
6. Handle other prayer requests from the phone calls.
7. Add your own prayer requests and comments to the notebook.

The costs for the prayer room were minimal — 144 keys, a telephone, and a prayer notebook! The most important costs were the commitment and dedication of the people.

I will never forget my first hour in the prayer room with my young family. It was an awesome experience. Our small children crawled up in our laps. Deana and Jeana are great prayer warriors to this day. It was the first time we had ever prayed for an hour together as a family! And, what a blessing it was to go to the prayer room week after week. Someone added sheets to the notebook that included prayer requests and prayers answered. I would always be overwhelmed by God's power when I left the prayer room.

> I would always be overwhelmed by God's power when I left the prayer room.

And God's power grew an old downtown church from 1200 to over 3,000! It did not happen until Broadway became a prayer-driven church!

When I was at Richland Hills in Fort Worth, Alvin Jennings led an effort to build a prayer garden next to the counseling center. Volunteer labor and community groups such as the boy scouts were responsible for much of the work. Thousands of people from the church and the community have used the outdoor prayer garden throughout the years.

Consider this: Could a prayer garden or something similar help your congregation?

The first thing you see as you approach the prayer garden is a curbside stone mailbox with "Praying Hands." The mailbox is for prayer requests and has a map of the prayer garden displayed. The Stone Arch serves as a beautiful entrance to the prayer garden. The Prayer Garden has over 1400 ft. of walking paths. The South Exit has a thicket of thorn bushes to remind people of the suffering of Jesus. The Empty Tomb represents the tomb from which Jesus was resurrected. Even the stone has been rolled away and the tomb looks so real. The Bridge is a reminder of others who have helped us on our journey to the heart of God. The Table will seat six people and is a good place for group prayer and meditation. The Memorial Wall was built in memory of Marcia Maserang who came to the Prayer Garden often to pray in her battle with cancer which was in remission for a long time. Prayer requests and comments may be left on cards provided here.

The midst of the garden is surrounded by huge stones which are used for seating during group prayer sessions or Bible lessons. Weddings and other special events have been conducted here. The Missions Memorial Pillar honors missionaries serving in various nations. The Pool of Bethesda reminds us of the power of God when an angel stirred the water in John 5. Many people have trod the Bridge to Golgotha beside the pool. It is the way to the cross of Jesus. The Hill of Golgotha has three crosses and chiseled into a rock are the "Seven Sayings of Jesus." Many kneel and pray here at the foot of the cross.

Prayer is remembering I am indispensable to God when I feel I'm only trash cluttering up the neighborhood.

The Garden of Prayer is located at 4921 Meadow Lakes Drive in North Richland Hills, Texas. Additional tracts and information about the Garden of Prayer are available from the Richland Hills Church of Christ, 6300 N.E. Loop 820. North Richland Hills, TX 76180 or Alvin Jennings, Star Bible Publications, Inc., P.O. Box 821220, Ft. Worth, TX 76182.

I love John Maxwell's books, but I believe the greatest book he has written is the one entitled *Partners in Prayer.* Ron Freeman gave me a copy of the book, and I have taught two series of lessons out of it. Ron is a shepherd at the Central Church of Christ and a great man of prayer. Ron has been battling lung cancer for a long time. Ron has really encouraged the prayer ministry at Central.

Please read *Partners in Prayer.* I have spoken several places where they have put the book into practice. It's overwhelming to have 50 to 100 people meet with you before morning services and place their hands on you and pray for you. Many of them express that they will be praying in the prayer room during the entire service for God's power to transform lives!

God raised up Dickie Haney in 1999 to coordinate the prayer ministry at Central. The Women's Prayer Ministry led by Emily Barber had been functioning marvelously for several years. But as the new millennium approached, it was time to join all our efforts into one great prayer ministry.

Point to ponder: How can you develop a prayer ministry in your congregation?

Dickie is a great man of prayer and utilized intensive, fervent prayer for his high school son, Luke, every night for four years. He also wrote a devotional guide for Luke as well as a prayer diary to give him at graduation.

Dickie and the Prayer Ministry turned a cry room into a prayer room complete with 18 chairs and a water fountain. The members of the prayer ministry pray during the services and see that each new member or convert has a prayer partner.

The following material comes from the Prayer Ministry led by Dickie Haney. It will show you how to organize and utilize a prayer ministry in your local church.

> It's overwhelming to have 50 to 100 people meet with you before morning services and place their hands on you and pray for you.

Central Church of Christ
Prayer Ministry

All great things begin with prayer! Without a doubt, Central is on the verge of greater things than we could ever imagine. As the love at Central continues to pour throughout Amarillo and the surrounding communities, it is vital that we maintain a strong and faithful foundation of prayer. You have volunteered to be an important part of a **"silent but very powerful prayer ministry."** For our prayer ministry to be successful, you are asked to provide:

✝ Daily Prayer
✝ Periodic Intensive Prayer
✝ Prayer during Worship Services
✝ Oversight of Weekly Prayer Requests

Daily Prayer

This is the most "open-spirited" method of prayer. When truly led by the Holy Spirit, we can effectively thank the Lord for his continuous blessings and cover the needs of the Central Family. Ask God for wisdom in interceding for the Church, its leaders, members, and our community. For the month of April, the following guidance can be used as general direction:

Weekday	Topic	Scripture
Sunday	*P* raise	Psalm 9:1-2
Monday	*R* esurrection	1 Corinthians 15
Tuesday	*A* ttitude	Philippians 2:1-11
Wednesday	*Y* outh	Titus 2:6-8
Thursday	*E* ncouragement	1 Thessalonians 4:16-18
Friday	*R* ejoice	Philippians 4:4-9
Saturday	*S* elf-control	1 Peter 4:7-11

Oversight of Weekly Prayer Requests

Toward the end of each service, prayer requests are gathered. Copies will be made and placed in the Prayer Room. At a convenient time please feel free to come by Central, spend time alone with Our Lord, and pray over these special needs.

Intensive Prayer

Leadership — Besides our daily intercession commit one

day of intensive prayer "without ceasing" in April for the leadership of Central (e.g., our elders, deacons, ministers, and staff). Our members will be prayerfully considering and submitting names for additional leaders. Our elders will be praying over the names and appointing these individuals during the month of May. Much prayer is needed on behalf of these individuals and their families, and the commitment required.

Sunday Morning Worship

Three April "Prayer Warriors" are needed to pray *for* our worship services *during* our worship services. These Warriors are as follows:

Date	Early Service Prayer Warriors	Late Service Prayer Warriors
04/04/99	_____	_____
	_____	_____
04/11/99	_____	_____
	_____	_____
04/18/99	_____	_____
	_____	_____
04/25/99	_____	_____
	_____	_____

Thought for the Month:

Once upon a time, a king had a boulder placed on a roadway. He hid himself and watched to see if anyone would remove the huge rock. Some of the king's wealthiest merchants came by and simply walked around it. Many loudly blamed the king for not keeping the roads clear, but none did anything about getting the big stone out of the way. Then a peasant came along carrying a load of vegetables. On approaching the boulder, he laid his burden down and tried to move the stone to the side of the road. After much pushing and straining, he finally succeeded. When the stone was moved, the peasant noticed a purse lying in the road where the boulder had been. In the purse were many gold coins and a note from the king promising the gold to the person who removed the boulder from the roadway. The peasant learned what many others never understood. Every obstacle presents an opportunity to improve one's condition.

We encounter boulders every day. These stones come in many sizes and different shapes. Sometimes they appear as pebbles of pride which must be pushed aside before we can continue down the path God has chosen for us. Other times, they resemble rocks of rebellion. If we can't have it our way, we'll not rest until we've made the path impass-able for everybody else. Sometimes they surface as stones of self-pity. We refuse to go on anymore and idly sit by until someone comes along and changes things for us. Jesus was laid in the tomb. A large stone was put at the entrance to keep him from going anywhere (Matt. 27:60-66). When the Sabbath was over, Mary Magdalene, Mary, the mother of James, and Salome were going to anoint Christ's body. They asked, "Who will roll the stone away from the entrance of the tomb?" But when they looked up, they saw that the stone, which was very large, had already been rolled away! (Mark 16:1-4). Who rolled the stone away? Take a guess. No stone's too big for God to move. The Lord moved 'em then. He can still move 'em today.

"Behold, I am coming soon! My reward is with me, and I will give to everyone according to what he has done" (Rev. 22:12).

"Lord, thanks for moving the stones we can't, and giving us the strength to move the ones we can."

Thanks for making a firm commitment to Central's Prayer Ministry, and . . .
"May the Lord continue to bless us well beyond our vision!!!"

(Sample prayer ministry newsletter, from April, 1999)

Central Church of Christ Prayer Ministry
Lead Prayer Warrior Responsibilities

Daily Prayer Coordinators

★ These individuals prepare topics and related Scriptures and submit them to the Prayer Newsletter Coordinators by the middle of each month.

Intensive Prayer Coordinators

★ These individuals coordinate with the staff, preachers and elders and inform the Calling Tree Coordinators of special needs and prayer requests.

Worship Prayer Coordinators

★ Each Sunday (at both services) these individuals:
- ✓ gather prayer requests during worship services;
- ✓ make two (2) copies;
- ✓ place one copy in the elders meeting room, and one copy in the prayer room
- ✓ place originals back in the auditorium.

Prayer Request Coordinators

★ These individuals obtain volunteers to pray **during** both services.

Calling Tree Coordinators

★ These individuals:
- ✓ form and maintain a current "calling tree" that includes everyone in this ministry;
- ✓ notify and update those on the "calling tree" of special needs and prayer requests when contacted by the Intensive Prayer Coordinators (or anyone else for that matter).

Prayer Newsletter Coordinator

★ These individuals prepare and submit the monthly newsletter that includes:
- ✓ topics and related Scriptures from the Daily Prayer Coordinators;
- ✓ special needs and prayer requests with updates;
- ✓ other information as deemed appropriate.

Prayer Room Designers

★ These individuals prepare the design and oversee the construction of the Prayer Room.

Prayer Room Carpenters

★ These individuals build the Prayer Room in strict accordance with the design and under the oversight of the Prayer Room Designers.

Prayer Room Administrators

★ These individuals verify the condition of the Prayer Room twice a week to ensure the facility is maintained.

Central Church of Christ
Prayer Ministry

The following are Prayer Ministry Assignments in need of Lead Warriors:

<u>Assignments</u>	<u>Lead Prayer Warriors</u>
Daily Prayer Coordinators	_____
	_____
Intensive Prayer Coordinators	_____
	_____
Worship Prayer Coordinators	_____
	_____
Prayer Request Coordinators	_____
	_____
Calling Tree Coordinators	_____
	_____
Prayer Newsletter Coordinators	_____
	_____
Prayer Room Designers	_____
	_____
Prayer Room Carpenters	_____
	_____
Prayer Room Administrators	_____
	_____

(Prayer ministry sign-up sheet)

Stay with me for a minute. You've lived a good life. The moment you've waited for has come at last! It's the Day of Judgment! You're at Heaven's Gates! The Lord turns to you, climbs deep in your heart and asks the question, **"Do you know you have accepted my Son?"** Without hesitation and with complete confidence you respond, **"Yes, Father."** He says, **"Welcome! You may now enter and go to the place that has been prepared for you" (John 14:2-4).** You turn to look back one last time and . . . Suddenly your heart stops! There he is — right behind you! Your eyes meet. He doesn't have to say anything. His eyes say it all, *"Why didn't you tell me about Jesus?"* You had many chances to share His story, share His love, but never found the courage. You try to ignore the flood of emotions that now overwhelm you: guilt, sorrow, regret. **"I'm going to heaven! Why dwell on the past."** But now it's too late.

Who was the person behind you? Was it someone you work with? went to school with? or possibly even someone you live with? Could it have made a difference if you would have said something but were too timid to talk? Perhaps the tragedy at the high school in Littleton, Colorado could've been avoided altogether if someone would've taken the time to share the love of our Lord with those students **before** they began loading their guns. We not only have the opportunity, but the responsibility to share His love. God's given us the ability to make a difference in the lives of those he's put in our path. It's not too late . . . yet.

Most of us can handle "major crises." It's the "daily whines" that can wear us completely out. Things like: computers going down; interstate construction; dead batteries; children going off to college; long lines in the checkout; call waiting; answering machines; voice mail; e-mail; on and on and on. (Sorry, I get a little carried away.) So, how do we handle the daily grind? James said it best in chapter 1:19-20: "Everyone should be quick to listen, slow to speak and slow to become angry, for man's anger does not bring about the righteous life that God desires."

"Rejoice in the Lord always. I will say it again: Rejoice! Let your gentleness be evident to all. The Lord is near. Do not be anxious about anything, but in everything, by prayer and petition, with thanksgiving, present your requests to God. And the peace of God, which transcends all understanding, will guard your hearts and your minds in Christ Jesus. Finally, brothers, whatever is true, whatever is noble, whatever is right, whatever is pure, whatever is lovely, whatever is admirable — if anything is excellent or praiseworthy — think about such things" (Phil. 4:4-8).

"Lord, there are so many times when our wants far outreach our needs. Thanks for Your patience when we whine. Keep us in the basket on those tough days. We never know which days we'll need You the most, so we ask that You watch over us every day. Help us to extend the same kindness to others that You so gently give to us. Help us to remember that You're always just a prayer away."

(Excerpts from the "Thought for the Month" in the May '99 and June '99 newsletters)

4 What Happens When Women Pray?

It seems that women in the early church placed great emphasis on prayer. Women were specifically listed with the apostles in the upper room praying in Acts 1. When Paul was looking for a place of prayer by a river in Acts 16, he found a group of WOMEN assembled there. He preached the gospel and Lydia

> Prayer always goes before revival.

became the first convert in Europe. When Paul addressed the church at Corinth, he states in 1 Corinthians 11:13 that women were supposed to pray with their heads covered.

Some church history books point out that women were especially involved in "prayer ministry" from A.D. 50 to 150. This especially became a major function of widows in the early church.

Prayer always goes before revival. The book entitled "America's Great Revivals" stresses this. Jonathan Edwards was a discouraged preacher in the 1730s. He was disgusted with the Halfway Covenant adopted by his religion that allowed people to be respectable "half way Christians." He built a tree house to pray alone as well as with his friends. He called for mothers and dads to put prayer back in their homes. A revival by Edwards began with six conversions. A notorious, young woman with a terrible, immoral reputation was one of the converts. Her conversion touched the lives of the young people all over the town and throughout the area. People gathered daily in their homes to pray. Within six months, 300 of the 1100 people in Northampton were converted. The revival spread to an additional hundred communities during the next six months. The revival became known as the "Great Awakening." Some history books suggest there were something like 50,000 conversions in the New England colonies from 1740 to 1760. The population of all the New England colonies at that time was only 340,000. The "Great Awakening" undoubtedly was a major cause for First Amendment support for religious liberty.

Another major revival began in New York City in 1858 and swept across America. It began with six people coming to a prayer meeting in New York City. It grew to 10,000 people daily gathering for prayer in New York City. There were 10,000 conversions in Philadelphia and over 150,000 people gathered to pray in a tent over a four-month period! For the entire United States, it is estimated there were over one million converts in the revival of 1858! The revival was the last great national revival in America.

One of the favorite stories told at the revival meetings across the country involved 25 women in the Midwest who got together once a week to pray for their unconverted husbands. Within six months, all 25 husbands had been converted!

On the first night of a revival in Kalamazoo, Michigan, in 1858, a woman wrote down a prayer request that stated: "A praying wife requests the prayers of this meeting for her unconverted husband, that he may be converted and made an humble disciple of the Lord Jesus. As soon as the preacher read this prayer request, a man came forward and said: "I am that man. I have a praying wife and this request must be for me." Four other men responded with the same requests. This started a revival that brought over 500 conversions!

Prayer is expecting a good crop from the barren fields watered only by my tears.

Think about it: What happens when wives pray for their husbands?

Women still seem to be the leaders in our prayer movements. I'm eternally grateful to my mother for

43

teaching me how to pray. I've done many surveys throughout the years and always find that more than 75% of our church leaders were taught to pray by their mothers. If you visit a Bible class of young children, you will normally have far more girls than boys wanting to lead the prayer!

Discuss this:
How does prayer change us? How does it change others?

When women pray today, God causes great change to take place. Prayer changes

> More than 75% of our church leaders were taught to pray by their mothers.

shirkers to workers,
pouters to shouters to God,
gripers to pipers of prayer!

Here are some of the major changes which take place:

1. It first changes the person praying. We are in closer touch with the spirit of Christ and the mind of God.
2. "Miraculous changes have taken place in the husbands.
3. "Impossible" situations with children have been changed.
4. Conversational prayer with husbands has greatly revived sexual fulfillment and communication.
5. Prayer partnership has brought great accountability to one another.
6. Prayer has given discipline to see the difference between wants and needs.
7. Prayer can eliminate harsh feelings.
8. Prayer brings peace of mind.
9. Prayer leads to hospital visits and contact with others who are needy.
10. Prayer brings encouraging notes to the bereaved.
11. Prayer makes meetings more effective.
12. Prayer brings revival to the church.

The Power of a Praying Wife by Stormie Omartian is an incredible book. She has another good book entitled *The Power of a Praying Mother*. Stormie stresses in her first book:

1. Prayer gets rid of power struggles in your marriage and invites God's power into your husband's life for his greatest blessings.

> Prayer gets rid of power struggles in your marriage

2. Change me to be the wife he needs—not change him, Lord.

3. Bless my husband's work so he will be fulfilled and can devote time to the family.

4. Help me to keep my husband happy sexually. Sex in marriage is God's idea and I want to get the most out of his plan.

5. Help me affirm my husband with words and actions which will increase his affection for me.

6. Protect my husband in temptation and relationships with other women.

7. Fill my husband's mind with good things and with the "fruit of the Spirit."

8. Give my husband peace and security as you protect him from fear.

9. Help my husband understand his purpose in life, and why God has called him "for such a time as this."

10. Give my husband special wisdom in all of the choices which he makes.

11. Please give my husband good health so he can fulfill your purposes for his life.

12. Please protect him from accidents, diseases, dangers and evil influences.

13. I don't even pretend to know all his trials, but God, provide him strength to overcome.

14. Help him always be a man of integrity.

15. Protect his reputation.

16. Bless his relationships with business associates and others with whom he has contact on a regular basis.

17. Help him be the father his children need.

18. Help him never feel like a failure, and help him live in the present instead of the past.

19. Regardless of the situation, help my husband always have a Christlike attitude.

45

20. Help our marriage to be all God wants it to be.
21. Emotions have their ups and downs. Help him to really trust me when he is down.
22. Help his walk and his talk glorify you and this family.
23. Help me be the person he comes to when he has made a mistake.
24. Give me the wisdom to help him when he needs help.
25. Help him read and follow God's word daily.
26. Help him understand that he was made in the image of God and help him to know that he is very, very special to me.
27. May his faith continue to grow.
28. Help him have a vision and a hope for his future. May he know that I want to spend eternity with him.[1]

Evelyn Christenson suggests the **6 "S's"** for women to follow in small group prayer time together.

> **S**ubject by subject — pray about one subject at a time.
> **S**hort prayers — only a few sentences from each person.
> **S**imple prayers.
> **S**pecific prayer requests.
> **S**ilent periods — where we reflect and listen because prayer is two-way conversation with God
> **S**mall groups which give people courage to pray.

The Prayer Hand is a good guide for us to follow when we pray alone. Each finger can provide us a guide to follow. The thumb is closest to our heart so pray for those closest to me. The forefinger

---

[1]*The Power of a Praying Wife* by Stormie Omartian. Copyright © 1997 by Harvest House Publishers, Eugene, Oregon 97402. Used by Permission.

represents those who teach me and point me to Christ. The tall middle finger represents those in leadership and authority. The next finger is the weakest finger, and it reminds us to pray for those who are weak. The small finger reminds me to pray for the little children as well as the need to pray for myself.

Women pray with such feeling and expression. I've always encouraged them to pray at our staff meetings. Their spirit makes a great impact on men.

It's sometimes frustrating when women don't know how to pray in women's classes, groups, etc. Every church needs a training program where godly women can teach other women to pray. I encourage women to pray in an organized way for 21 consecutive days because 21 days makes a habit.

> Women pray with such feeling and expression.

Women are great at taking outlines such as the one for the book of Lamentations and praying together in groups.

Chapter 1—Tears for "the City." (Pray for your city, town or community.)

Chapter 2—Tears for "the daughter of Zion." (Pray for the daughters.)

Chapter 3—Tears for "the man who has seen affliction." (Pray for your husband and other troubled men.)

Chapter 4—Tears for "the precious sons of Zion." (Pray for the sons.)

Chapter 5—Tears for "the orphans and fatherless." (Pray for those in broken and troubled homes.)

Try this exercise: Write out a sample prayer following this outline.

Women are extremely good at praying through the Bible. Here is a suggested outline to follow:

Genesis — Begin each day with God.

Exodus — Come out of negative environments to follow God.

Leviticus — Get right with God.

Numbers — Get somewhere with God.

Deuteronomy — Stop and think.

Joshua — Spiritually conquer your problems.

Judges — Discipline yourself and watch the boundaries.

Ruth — Gather the blessings and let God restore you.

1 Samuel — Light the altar lamps and pray.

2 Samuel — Be God's anointed.

1 Kings — You reap what you sow.

2 Kings — Try to turn a nation back to God

1 Chronicles — Follow the royal line.

2 Chronicles — Honor the King.

Ezra — Repair God's house.

Nehemiah — Rebuild God's City.

Esther — Trust God's grace.

Job — Let God have his way with you.

Psalms — Pray and Praise (God's servant on his knees).

Proverbs — Walk and work (God's servant on his feet).

Ecclesiastes — Fear God and be wise.

Song of Solomon — Love God with all your heart.

Isaiah — He is coming!

Jeremiah — Get ready with cleansing of the heart.

Lamentations — Get ready with weeping.

Ezekiel — Restore the temple.

Daniel — Bless the Kingdom.

Hosea — Return to God.

Joel — Sound the alarm.

Amos — Drop the plumb line.

Obadiah — Possess your possessions.

Jonah — Follow God's instructions.

Micah — Look and live.

Nahum — The mountains shake.

Habakkuk — But there's a light up ahead.

Zephaniah — Sing as you go.

Haggai — Work as you go.

Zechariah — The Lord will bring comfort.

Malachi — Listen to his messenger.

Matthew — The Messiah has come.

Mark — His marvelous works prove him.

Luke — He is a friend of sinners.

John — He is the Son of God.

Acts — He is at God's right hand for us.

Romans — Come to him for grace and righteousness.

1 Corinthians — Thank him for your spiritual gifts.

2 Corinthians — Thank him for comforts and blessings.

Galatians — Thank him for freedom and power.

Ephesians — Thank him for fullness of life.

Philippians — Thank him for joy.

Colossians — Thank him for making your life complete.

1 Thessalonians — He is coming again.

2 Thessalonians — Wait and work until he comes.

1 Timothy — Guard the gospel.

2 Timothy — Guard the witnesses of the gospel.

Titus — Adorn the doctrine.

Philemon — Be kind to everyone for his sake.

Hebrews — He is our intercessor at the throne.

James — Good works follow his way.

1 Peter — He is precious to those who believe.

2 Peter — He is gracious and glorious to those who believe.

1 John — He is the life.

2 John — He is the truth.

3 John — He is the way.

Jude — He can keep me from stumbling.

Revelation — He wants to welcome me to heaven.

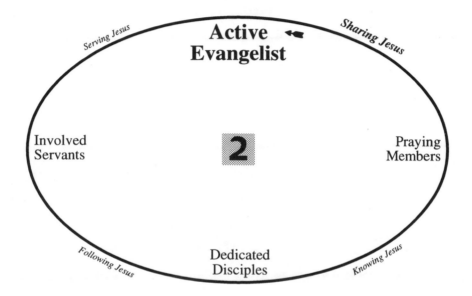

Prayer Is the Foundation of Evangelism

For the first quarter mile, we have stressed the importance of **Praying Members** knowing Jesus. We shared four chapters suggesting ways to do this. Now we are ready for our members to be **Active Evangelists** sharing Jesus. Our new people are excited about the gospel and they have friends who are lost in the world. They may not know a lot of doctrine at this point, but they do know how to share their story of why they became a Christian. They know how to pray, and they will pray by name for the lost. The new Christians in the early church "turned the world upside down" for Jesus Christ. We have looked at

> New converts may not know a lot of doctrine, but they know how to share their own story.

the book of Acts and seen how this evangelistic model in the early church was powered by prayer. We have made evangelism far too complicated in the modern world and have neglected the model for evangelism in the early church. Many of these "unschooled, ordinary men and women" (Acts 4:13) became extraordinary soul winners for Jesus Christ, and the "Lord added to the church daily" (Acts 2:47). Those who had been scattered because of persecution taught the gospel wherever they went (Acts 8:4).

I believe that prayer always precedes evangelism. In fact, I am a product of prayer evangelism. I never went to Bible school the first six years of my life. In fact, I had never even heard of Bible school. But in a first grade Bible class at the Kirkland Church of Christ, a teacher by the name of Mrs. Holleman encouraged

Do this:
Share your own story of why you are a Christian.

51

her students to pray for their friends who might come to Bible school. I didn't know any of this was happening, but a boy by the name of Johnny was praying for me. While he was in the first grade class with me at public school, he invited me to Bible school. I didn't know what Bible school was, but Johnny was excited about it and convinced me that I should come. We lived far out in the country so I rode the school bus each day. When I arrived home, I ran up to Mother and Dad and said, "Will you take me to Bible School Sunday?" Of course, they agreed to do this. This was during the month of February when I was in the first grade. On Sunday morning, we pulled up in front of a building that had Kirkland Church of Christ written on the outside of it. We trudged up the steps to the main auditorium and then down the steps to the basement for my class. Guess who my teacher was? She was the same teacher I had in public school! When I arrived in class, Johnny was so excited. I learned later that he got a prize for getting me to come!

I got off to a great start in class and everyone was so friendly. The teacher did the archaic practice of calling the class roll. She had a poster board chart on the wall for attendance. By the side of the name of all of those present, she put a gold star. By the names of the absentees, she placed a black star. We came the next three or four weeks and everything was going great. Then, we missed three weeks, and I will never forget coming back to class. The first thing you would see when you walked into class was the attendance chart. There were three ugly, black stars by the side of my name. I'm an only child, and I started screaming as loudly as I could! I ran up to the main auditorium class where Mom and Dad were! I kept screaming black star! Black star! I pulled Mom

> Prayer is remembering that my greatest blessing is His presence with me.

Think about it:
What can you learn from your own early experiences with Bible School?

and Dad down the steps to show them the attendance chart.

To make a long story short, we didn't even stay for Bible school or church that Sunday morning. My parents had to get that "screaming kid" home! But, as soon as the last Amen was said, the preacher, Eldon Sanders drove all the way out to our home in the country. He spent the rest of the afternoon teaching the Bible to Mom and Dad. This led to their conversion! There are a lot of simple steps in this plan of evangelism that opened the door for my salvation.

1. A teacher encouraging students to pray for friends who were not coming to Bible school.
2. An invitation to come by a student.
3. A friendly class.
4. An attendance chart.
5. A caring minister who drove out to our home and taught the word of God. (The best ministers still make house calls.)

All of this helped lead to my conversion at the age of 12. I also started preaching at the age of 12! I'll never forget my first sermon. I had worked on the lesson for a long time and practiced for hours before a mirror. I thought the lesson would last 20 minutes, but it barely lasted five minutes. Lo and behold, an older lady came forward at the invitation to be baptized! I had not practiced how to baptize anyone, and I nearly drowned her in the baptistery!

> The best ministers still make house calls.

On the way home from church, I was feeling on "top of the world." This sermon must have been incredible, and I wanted to preach it everywhere. At lunch that day, Dad prayed for the woman by name who had been baptized. It then dawned on me that Dad had been praying for her by name to obey the gospel! He had been doing this for over six months! He worked with her on his job, and they had been studying the Bible together at noon each day! My lesson had nothing to do with her obeying the gospel. She had told Dad she was going to be baptized that day! What a great lesson I learned in humility!

Producing active evangelists has been one of the greatest weaknesses in the church in recent years. There is no doubt that God wants us to produce active evan-

> God can't steer a parked car.

gelists. We need to do God's work in God's way for God's glory. But God can't steer a parked car! We'll look at a ministry I call "Caring Ministry" as a way to help us. "Caring Ministry" is probably not for every church, but it gives us the opportunity to get a church MOVING in a great effort to reach the lost. It begins as a ministry where each person is trained to fulfill important tasks and responsibilities. It grows to spiritual maturity when "my ministry" only becomes ministry when something happens to someone else's heart as a result of God working through me. The great news becomes: I really don't have a ministry, I AM ONE!

"Caring Ministry" for the 21st century begins with prayer and the Vision, Mission, and Values of the local church. Every member should have input in this process. After this information has been turned in to the leadership, a leadership retreat should produce Vision, Mission, and Values statements. Always begin first by formulating the values. This Vision, Mission, and Values statements should now be shared with the congregation to provide a compass for the direction of the church. If this statement stresses evangelism, and church leaders are united in this effort — the congregation is a good candidate for the "Caring Ministry."

Caring Ministry tries to change a "maintenance church" to a "mission church" to reach the lost. This can be very difficult to do. Some surveys show that 95% of church members never bring anyone to Christ outside of members of their immediate family. Pray that God will work mightily among you as you deal with the following changes.

Caring Ministry tries to change a "maintenance church" to a "mission church" to reach the lost.

1. When you change the values and priorities, you change the church.
2. When you change the church calendar and scheduled events, you change the church.
3. When you change the Bible classes, you change the church.
4. When you change the worship styles, you change the church.
5. When you change the small groups, you change the church.
6. When you change the prayer emphasis, you change the church.

This dream of changing a "maintenance church" to a "mission church" was shared with the Central Church of Christ in Amarillo on the first Sunday of November, 1998. Approximately 250 people responded at the invitation! They were excited about this new emphasis and spent the rest of the day in training to implement these new principles.

Ask yourself: Why is it so hard to change a maintenance church to a mission church?

Caring Ministry emphasizes first-time attendees. The average church only reaches 10-15% of their first-time attendees. If that percentage could be changed to 85%, it would foster a lot of growth for the local church. We set up a first-time attendees parking lot with a large banner next to the building. We also reserved another visitors lot. It is a good idea to use the church youth to wash the windshields of the cars in the First Time Attendees and visitors parking lots. Leave a sheet under the windshield wiper which says: "This windshield was washed by the youth at this church. Thanks for being here, and may God bless your week. We are praying for you to visit with us again." Trained care ministry teams know how to recognize first-time attendees, and they ask them three questions:

1. What is your name?

For your consideration: What kinds of questions or statements do you use in greeting visitors?

2. How long have you been attending here?
3. Could I pray with you about some need?

These contacts may take place in the parking lot, foyer or back of the auditorium. We also encourage them to fill out prayer request cards. The opening welcome announcement for visitors contains these words: "We believe visitors do not come by accident — but by divine appointment. We have been praying for you to visit with us, and we believe God has answered our prayers. We believe God brought you to us because He wants us to minister to your needs." We have had phenomenal results. We are currently averaging 45 first-time attendees and the number of prayer requests has grown from 10 to 50!

> We believe visitors do not come by accident — but by divine appointment.

We try to get all of the first-time attendees to a hospitality booth to meet elders and ministers. We also try to get them in a Sunday morning class and Sunday night small group. We also try to take every first-time attendee out to eat.

We make seven contacts with these visitors during the next seven days:

Monday   Cookies taken to their home.
Tuesday   Staff person calls to say we are praying for them.
Wednesday   Letter from minister and invitation to Welcome Class
Thursday   Care Team Leader calls.
Friday   Receive church brochure and information about classes.
Saturday   Phone call reminder and invitation to sit with them or provide transportation for them if they need a ride.

The Welcome Class is a perpetual class that is conducted on Sunday morning or Wednesday night. Every four weeks the first-time attendees in the Welcome Class eat in the preacher's home!

We followed this with strategic planning for our divine appointments. We challenged our ministries to list ways they could produce First Time Attendees and meet their needs. We used our fifteen Sunday morning classes to train our people for personal evangelism for the next thirteen weeks. Since the average class member knows about twenty unchurched people, we challenged each member to designate Amarillo as their mission field and to list the names of twenty people they would pray for daily. We also changed our Wednesday night classes to provide entry level classes for nonmembers, average level classes, many training classes in outreach and in-depth Bible school classes for the spiritually mature. We scheduled special outreach services for Easter and had nearly 3,000 present as a culmination of our planning. This was an incredible spiritual experience!

> Prayer is remembering I carry God's awesome presence into each daily encounter.

Despite the success, let me share with you some things that are very difficult as we strive to change a "maintenance church" to a "mission church."

1. It was hard to integrate outsiders into our Sunday night groups.
2. It was difficult to blend them into our Sunday morning classes.
3. Some of our Sunday morning classes did not like thirteen weeks of personal evangelism lessons.
4. Some members complained about their needs not being met.
5. Parking is always at a premium; some members complained about this.
6. Some complained about thirteen weeks of sermons on evangelism.
7. Some wanted more in-depth lessons.
8. Some disliked giving up the back rows in the auditorium for visitors.

For your own situation: What practical ways can each of these problems be addressed?

9. Some wanted to "do their own thing" in class.
10. Some complained about so many care ministry members being up and meeting visitors during services.

Consider carefully: Is caring ministry for your congregation?

Caring Ministry is *not* for every congregation. There must first be the desire to change from a "maintenance church" to a "mission church." There must be adequate training and follow-up.

But, Caring Ministry could be the answer to your prayers!

The "Caring Ministry" produced major changes for our church services and classes. We came up with an overall plan for our major priorities. It looks like this:

Central Church of Christ
"A Place to Call Home"

Fulfilling God's Purpose
Meeting Your Needs

Sunday Morning	Sunday Night	Wednesday Night
Caring	Connecting	Equipping
Inspiring	Involving	Discipling
Rest	of	Week
Praying	Bible Study	Serving

Every 5th Sunday

All Together Fellowship
Special Event
Leadership
Cluster Meetings

"If anyone would come after me, he must deny himself and take up his cross daily and follow me" (Luke 9:23).

Notice the diagram is shaped like a cross because we want everyone to focus on Jesus, and we want to encourage prayer in the spirit of kneeling at the foot of the cross. Our two overall goals involved:

Fulfilling God's purpose.
Meeting people's needs.

Our Sunday morning priorities were a "Caring Ministry" for evangelism and First-Time Attendees along with the goal of inspiring every member to follow Jesus. On Sunday night, we were interested in connecting our people with one another with an emphasis on small groups and involving people in ministry. Our Wednesday night program stressed Equipping as we trained people, and we also offered more in-depth Discipling Classes. We encouraged people throughout the week to PRAY, study and serve. Every fifth Sunday we planned an All Together Service and Fellowship. This would be centered around a special event. Leadership spiritual cluster meetings were planned for Sunday afternoons.

> We want everyone to focus on Jesus.

Your priorities will probably be different, but let me encourage you to look at Sunday morning, Sunday night, Wednesday night, etc. — and come up with special purposes and priorities for these times. Your people deserve to know what the major goals are and this can be a big winner with them.

Planning for your situation: What new or different classes should your congregation offer?

After we got our "Caring Ministry" underway, it made major changes in our Wednesday night curriculum. We went to four different levels of classes. The 100 level classes were for nonmembers and new members. Before we added these classes, we had no place for these people on Wednesday nights.

The 200 level classes were average classes similar to those we had been having on Wednesday nights. The 300 level classes were training and equipping classes. These classes were of vital importance because we needed to provide a lot of training for all of the new things we were doing.

The 400 level classes were in-depth classes. These classes were especially needed because we were using all of our Sunday morning classes to train people in personal evangelism and first principles. (See next page, illustration 1, for the class list.)

One of the important classes to offer is a Welcome Class for new members and potential members who want to learn more about you. It can be offered on Wednesday night, Sunday night or Sunday morning. (Illustration 2a shows a welcome letter for this class.)

It is a good idea for the pulpit minister to at least teach the first session of this class. Elders and other ministers can also help out. We run the class perpetually for four weeks. New people can enter the class at any time. The fourth week is always a meal in the preacher's home. This is an overwhelming success. Be sure elders and wives are present for this meal with the new members. Provide plenty of house cleaning and cooking help for the minister and his wife.

Point to Ponder:
What special events or programs do you have for newcomers?

The material on the next few pages show some of the things we cover in the Welcome Class. (Adapt these for your own use.) We want our new *Prayer is the way to please God.* members to be prayers. We want them ing, informed mem- (see illustrations 2b to make friends we want them to through 2d). And, invite their friends who are outside the church. Be sure to include the Quarter Mile Chart (illustration 2g has one form of this) in your handouts and discussions with them. They need to know where the church is going. The Vision, Mission, and Values Statements also need to be discussed with them. You might also consider using the Spiritual Gifts Inventory we showed in our previous book, *The Servant Driven Church*, available as a 4-page brochure from Guidance Assistance Programs, PO Box 105, Winfield, IL 60190. One essential inclusion is a list of adult Bible Classes, complete with meeting place and teacher.

It's Coming This Sunday!

Welcome Class

This is a special four-week class for people who are new members and visitors at Central. You will meet new people, hear what's happening at Central, and learn what it means to be a member.

The fourth week of class we will all be having dinner at the home of Dick and Lou Nell Marcear. It will be a fun evening.

In the past, we have held the Welcome Class on Wednesday evenings . . . but this prevented a number from coming. Our new format will be on Sunday morning. Here are the details:

PLACE: Fireplace Room

TIME: 9:45 - 10:45 a.m.

CHILDREN: There is a full lineup of classes for kids, plus the nursery will be open.

ATMOSPHERE: The class is held in a very informal atmosphere. There is no pressure of any kind put on anyone. You can feel free to invite anyone you wish to be in class.

Week 1 — You will learn about Central's history and her dreams for the future.

Week 2 — You will meet many new people and form some wonderful friendships.

Week 3 — You will learn who we are, what we stand for, and what is expected of one who is a member at Central.

Week 4 — You will be invited to the Marcears' home for dinner one evening and that's always fun.

WEDNESDAY NIGHT
BIBLE CLASSES FOR ADULTS

100 Level Classes (Entry Level)

Fireplace Room	Welcome Class	Dick Marcear
B-G	New Life Class	Bill Snow
	(Learning to Be a Follower of Jesus)	

200 Level Classes (Regular Classes)

Chapel	"What Rules Your Life?"	Carroll Thomason
B-35	Discussion Class	Jim Hays

300 Level Classes (Training)

B-K	Care Ministry	Bob Crass
New Fellowship	Teacher Training	Ray Fulenwider
Old Fellowship	Singing Class	Lee Kendle
B-D	"True Love Waits"	Kyle Meador
	(for **parents** of children & teens)	
B-F	Parenting of Toddlers	Cayce & Patrice Powell
B-37	Divorce Care	Wib Newton
B-36, J, H, L	Kids Care	

400 Level Classes (In-depth)

B-30	Scheme of Redemption	Warlick Thomas
B-M	1 Corinthians	Leon Wood

Illustration 1

10 MOST WANTED LIST

The rules of the game are very simple. See if you can find 10 people who fit the description of each category. Do not use any person's name twice. Try to talk to every person in the room. You will have 10 minutes.

1. Someone who has traveled outside the 48 states in the past year: _____

2. A girl who played sports in high school: _____

3. Someone whose father was/is a preacher or an elder: _____

4. Someone raised in a large family (most number of kids): _____

5. Someone who has lived in Amarillo 9 weeks or less: _____

6. Someone who was an only child: _____

7. Someone who owns a boat, motorcycle, VW, jet ski or ATV: _____

8. Someone who has visited the Bible lands: _____

9. Someone who can say the books of the New Testament: _____

10. Someone who has a funny story or joke that they would like to share with us: _____

Friendship: The Priceless Gift

One of the purposes of our class is to get to know new people and make some new friends. To help us get to know each other better, we will be playing a game. In 10 minutes see if you can find people who fit the following descriptions. No name can be used twice. Write the name of the person you find in the blank.

1. Someone who has a motor home, travel trailer . . . or tent _____

2. Someone whose father was a minister, elder or deacon _____

3. Someone with a birthday in the same month as yours _____

4. Someone wearing the same color dress, shirt, pants, etc. _____

5. Someone who isn't married _____

6. Someone who has lived east of the Mississippi River _____

7. Someone who has been a Bible school teacher _____

8. Someone born in a state other than Texas _____

9. Someone who has a unique pet; what is it? _____

10. Someone who has lived in Amarillo six months or less _____

HISTORY OF THE CENTRAL CHURCH OF CHRIST

AMARILLO'S HISTORY

1. September 8, 1887 — first train came to Amarillo
2. 1890–1900 — population grew from 483 to 1442
   (In 1899 all men, 18–45, were required to work 8 hours a day to lay bricks for city streets — paid $1.00 a day.)
3. 1904 — first car came to Amarillo
4. 1908 — population reached almost 8,000.

CENTRAL'S HISTORY

1. October 2, 1908 — people gathered in Potter County Courthouse to form the Central Church of Christ. Joe Banman, traveling preacher from Gainesville preached the first sermon.
2. 1909 — F.L. YOUNG became the first regular preacher: Frame building purchased at corner of 6th & Filmore.
3. 1911 — F.B. SHEPHERD became Central's minister.
4. 1916 — church had grown and new building built at 10th and Filmore.
5. 1928 — fireball, ROBERT C. JONES and lovely wife LOIS came to Central. Probably the most influential preacher in Central's history.
6. 1929 — not good year in Panhandle. 1930-1935 days known as "Dust Bowl Days." Church leaders & members had great faith. Bought land and decided to build new building at 15th & Monroe. Cost? $100,000 (during Great Depression).
7. Building committee (H.L. ADKINS, J.B. RATLIFF, G.W. MILLS & A.B. JONES) rode the train to Dallas to see the building of the Oakcliff C. of C. It was inspiration and model for the Central building. The Oakcliff building no longer remains.
8. Last service held at 10th & Filmore, April 20, 1930. From then until October 19, 1930 church met in the Old Presbyterian building at 10th & Tyler.
9. October 19, 1930 — first meeting in Central's Chapel. ROBERT C. JONES preached first sermon.
10. Over the years, since 1908, Central has been served by 17 ministers. Dick Marcear came to Centr:1 in 1975.

FIND THE RIGHT NUMBER

The object of this game is to find someone who fits in each of these ten categories. When you find a person who fits, write in his/her name in the blank. Please use a person's name only once. Good luck!

1. SOMEONE WHO WAS AN ONLY CHILD _____

2. SOMEONE WHO HAS TWO CHILDREN _____

3. SOMEONE WHO HAS LIVED IN AT LEAST 3 STATES _____

4. SOMEONE WHO WAS RAISED IN A FAMILY WITH AT LEAST FOUR KIDS _____

5. SOMEONE WHO HAS FIVE PETS _____

6. SOMEONE WHO CAN NAME SIX APOSTLES _____

7. SOMEONE WHO WAS BORN IN A STATE WITH AT LEAST SEVEN LETTERS _____

8. SOMEONE WHO HAS LIVED AT LEAST 800 MILES FROM AMARILLO _____

9. SOMEONE WHO HAS LIVED IN AMARILLO NINE WEEKS OR LESS _____

10. SOMEONE WHO HAS LEARNED THE FIRST NAME OF TEN PEOPLE IN OUR CLASS _____

"My house will be called a house of prayer" (Matt. 21:13).
"After they prayed, the place where they were meeting was shaken. And they were all filled with the Holy spirit and spoke the word of God boldly" (Acts 4:31).

Serving Jesus	Acts 2:47; Mark 16:15-16	*Sharing Jesus*

Active Evangelist
2nd quarter

Acts 2:45; 1 Peter 4:10	**Four Quarters in a**	Acts 2:42; Matthew 7:7
Involved Servants	**One-Mile Racetrack**	**Praying Members**
3rd quarter		*1st quarter*

John 13:34-35; 1 Corinthians 3:1-9;
Acts 4:32-35

Following Jesus	Dedicated Disciples	*Knowing Jesus*
	1 Mile	

"I do not run like a man running aimlessly" (1 Cor. 9:26).
"Let us run with perseverance the race marked out for us. Let us fix our eyes on Jesus, the author and perfecter of our faith" (Heb. 12:1-2).
"I have finished the race, I have kept the faith. Now there is in store for me the crown of righteousness" (2 Tim. 4:7-8).

Central Church of Christ
Third Millennium

Vision (Where we're going.)
Our Vision is to be: **"An Exciting Place to Call Home"**

Mission (What we do.)
Our Mission is to: **"Attract All People to a Relationship with Jesus"**

Values (Who we are.)

We Believe:

1. *The Bible is the inspired word of God and is our final authority in all matters.*
2. *Each member is to use his gifts for the glory of God.*
3. *Every soul is of immeasurable value to God.*
4. *We are to accept one another just as God has accepted us.*
5. *We are stewards of all God has given us.*
6. *God wants all believers to be one in Christ.*
7. *The "Great Commandment" defines our primary love.*
8. *The "Great Commission" is our charge from Jesus.*
9. *We are to have the "attitude of Christ."*
10. *God answers prayer.*
11. *We are saved by the grace of God.*
12. *The Trinity (Father, Son & Holy Spirit).*

HOW IS CENTRAL ORGANIZED?

1 Timothy 3:1-13

CHURCH IS LED BY ELDERS/OVERSEERS

Qualifications are given in 1 Timothy 3:2-7 (Titus 1:5-9).

We have 13 elders:

Rusty Burns	Frank Stepp
Bob Crass	Mike Robinson
Ron Freeman	Al Smith
Bill Johnson	Craig Gladman
John Noyes	Warlick Thomas
Steve Rogers	Leon Wood
Shelby Stapleton	

*Bob Crass and Shelby Stapleton are full-time elders who deal with shepherding, small groups, and management.

NOTE: The elders meet regularly at 8:15 p.m. on Wednesday evenings. The chairmanship is rotated on a three month basis. The elders are always open for people who would like to meet with them for prayer. If possible contact the chairman before, but if not, just come to the Assembly Room (near chapel) at 8 o'clock.

CENTRAL IS SERVED BY ABOUT 80 DEACONS — 1 Timothy 3:8-13

THE CHURCH STAFF IS MADE UP OF MEN AND WOMEN WHO SERVE IN DIFFERENT AREAS:

1. Ray Fulenwider — Education/Involvement
2. Jordan Hubbard — Youth
3. Becky Kelly — Children
4. Dick Marcear — Pulpit
5. Kyle Meador — Media/Discipleship
6. Wib Newton — Family/Counseling
7. Paul Sneed — Hospitals/Funerals
8. Bill Snow — Singles
9. Carroll Thomason — Senior Adults
10. Lee Kindle — Music
11. Stephanie Alvarado — Children
12. Kathi Haynes — Children
13. Kayla Middleton — Kid's Universe

We are supported by a wonderful staff of ladies who work in our office:

Pat Dye	Diane Venegoni
Connie Green	Janie Weems
Celia Tidmore	Karen Williams

THE REAL WORK IS DONE BY OUR MANY VOLUNTEERS.

Illustration 2h

CENTRAL CHURCH OF CHRIST

Date: _____ Marital Status: ___ M ___ S ___ D ___ W

Last Name: _____

Home Address: _____

Mailing Address, if different: _____

Home Phone: _____

Business Phone: Head of House: _____

    Name of Employer: _____

    Spouse: _____

    Name of Employer: _____

FAMILY INFORMATION

	First Name	Birthdate	Grade	Baptized
Head of Household				
Spouse				
Child (male/female)				
Child (male/female)				
Child (male/female)				
Child (male/female)				
Child (male/female)				
Child (male/female)				

Other relatives at Central: _____

Do you attend Sunday morning Bible Class? _____
Which class? _____

Do you attend Wednesday evening Bible Class? _____
Which class? _____

Ministry Sign Up

Name _____

Adult Class _____

Home Phone _____ WorkPhone _____

☐ 1. Adult Recreation
☐ 2. Attendance Reports
☐ 3. Baptismal Assistance
☐ 4. Bible Hour
☐ 5. Bible Quiz
☐ 6. Building Maintenance
☐ 7. Calling and Caring
☐ 8. Care Ministry
☐ 9. Children's Recreation & Fellowship
☐ 10. Children's Singing & Drama
☐ 11. Christian Camps & Retreats
☐ 12. Church Growth
☐ 13. College
☐ 14. Communications
☐ 15. Community Care
☐ 16. Community Outreach
☐ 17. Contribution
☐ 18. Dorcas & Timothy
☐ 19. Education — Adult
☐ 20. Education — Children
☐ 21. Education — Youth
☐ 22. Evangelistic Small Group
☐ 23. Family Camps
☐ 24. Family Life Groups
☐ 25. Finance
☐ 26. Good Samaritan
☐ 27. Greeters
☐ 28. Hall Monitors
☐ 29. High Plains Children's Hour
☐ 30. Hospital Visitation
☐ 31. Huddles — High School
☐ 32. Involvement
☐ 33. Lighting & Sound
☐ 34. Lord's Table Service
☐ 35. Missions
☐ 36. New Member Assimilation
☐ 37. Nursery & Child Care
☐ 38. Personal Finance
☐ 39. Prayer
☐ 40. Prison & Jail Ministry
☐ 41. Sojourners
☐ 42. Special Events
☐ 43. Sunshiners
☐ 44. Tape Ministry
☐ 45. Transportation
☐ 46. Visitation
☐ 47. Visitation, Special
☐ 48. Welcome Home
☐ 49. Young Couples
☐ 50. Youth

Tell us about ourselves

1. Are you a member at Central? ___ Yes ___ No If yes, how long? ___

2. Are you enrolled in an adult Bible class? ___ Yes ___ No

3. What brought you to Central? ___

4. What was your first impression of us? ___
   What made you feel that way? ___

5. How could we improve our:
   A. Worship services ___
   B. Bible school program ___
   C. New members class ___

6. What could we do to make new members feel more "at home"? ___

7. What could we do to be more effective in bringing in new members? ___

8. What have we not covered that you would like to know more about? ___

9. Which service do you usually attend?
   8:30 ___ 11:00 ___

10. Other than your friends, what one thing would you like to have brought to Central with you? ___

11. What do you think is/was the best and weakest part of our New Members class? Best class? ___
    Weakest? ___

12. What do you like best about Central? ___

SKILLS INVENTORY SECTION

Teaching experience — check area(s) in which you have taught or are currently teaching.

BIBLE CLASS TEACHING EXPERIENCE

A. ___ Nursery (0-6 mo.)   H. ___ Senior High (9th-12th grade)
B. ___ Nursery (6-12 mo.)   I. ___ College
C. ___ Nursery (12-18 mo.)   J. ___ Singles
D. ___ Nursery (18-24 mo.)   K. ___ Adult
E. ___ Preschool (2-5 yrs.)   L. ___ Ladies' Bible Class
F. ___ Elementary (1st-5th gr.) M. ___ Vacation Bible School
G. ___ Middle School (6th-8th gr.) N. ___ Home Bible Studies

Would you be willing to teach? ___ What level? ___
Willing to attend teacher-training program? ___
Willing to assist in making visual aids? ___
Willing to work in Resource Room? ___
Do you have experience in counseling? ___ Degree? ___
Any college hours in counseling? ___

WORSHIP — Check area(s) of worship where you would be willing to serve if called upon:

___ Preach   ___ Help Serve Communion
___ Lead Singing   ___ Officiate at Communion Table
___ Lead Prayer   ___ Sing for Special Occasions
                            (weddings, funerals, etc.)

Do you sing: Soprano ___ Alto ___ Tenor ___ Bass ___

SPECIAL SKILLS: Please read through the brochure which describes the aims and service possibilities of each ministry. Do you have a special skill that would benefit any particular ministry? Which ministry? ___
What is your special skill? ___

The best time for a congregation to grow is from January through Easter each year. The following lessons were taught in all of our Sunday morning classes during this period of time. We used our classes like evangelistic training classes with special outreach to visitors.

We asked for each class member to claim Amarillo, Texas, as "My Mission Field" and to list the names of unchurched people they knew on their prospect list. Instructions about praying for people on the prospect list were also included.

> The best time for a congregation to grow is from January through Easter each year.

Try this: Track on a calendar when you have had your ups and downs in attendance. Do you make proper use of special occasions like Easter?

My Mission Field

This page is a card approximately 5½" × 8½". One side has a place to list the names, addresses, and phone numbers of 20 friends to be prayed for and evangelized and the following Scripture: "Ask and it will be given to you; seek and you will find; knock and the door will be opened to you" (Matt. 7:7).

The other side contains the following text:

PRAYING FOR THE PEOPLE ON YOUR IMPACT LIST

Begin to pray for the people on your *Impact List.* Ask God to work in their lives and to give you wisdom on how to effectively reach out to them. In praying for them keep in mind the following three areas:

Them

Ask God to:
- ◆ Pull them toward Himself
- ◆ Open their eyes to the emptiness of life without Him
- ◆ Help them see their need for forgiveness
- ◆ Remove the confusion they have about Him and the life He offers
- ◆ Help them grasp the meaning and importance of the cross of Christ
- ◆ Open the person's heart to God's love and truth

You

Ask God to:
- ◆ Help you live a consistent and attractive Christian life

- Make you authentic and honest as you deal with life's ups and downs
- Give you wisdom in knowing how to approach the relationship
- Expand your knowledge so you will be ready to define and defend the gospel message
- Help them grasp the meaning and importance of the cross of Christ
- Grant you appropriate boldness and courage
- Use you to help lead this person into a relationship with Christ

Us

Ask God to:
- Cause depth and trust to grow in the relationship
- Open doors for spiritual conversations
- Guide those conversations in pace, frequency, and content

Our climax for all of these activities was Easter Sunday when we had a traditional outreach service at 8:30 a.m. and a contemporary outreach service at 11:00 a.m. Our teenagers worked for months on an exciting outreach drama entitled "Broadcast of the Crucifixion." The Crucifixion was presented like live television reports complete with video cameras, large screens, special effects, etc. This outstanding drama served as our 9:45 a.m. Bible class for adults and youth. We also presented the

---

Sleep an extra hour
don't change your clocks until you join us.

Easter Sunday, April 4
for inspirational & spiritual worship

8:30 a.m.   *Where Is the Lamb?* — a traditional worship service

9:45 a.m.   "Broadcast of the Crucifixion" — a three-act production
(held in our basement fellowship hall)

11:00 a.m.   *Act of Love* — a contemporary worship service

Communion offered during both worship services.

Illustration 3a

> **The Exciting**
> **Central Church of Christ**
> **15th & Monroe**
> **Dick Marcear, Minister**
>
> ***An exciting place to call home!***
> with ministries for . . .
> ◆ families
> ◆ singles
> ◆ children
> ◆ senior adults
> ◆ youth
> and so much more . . .
>
> Contact us for details about our
> worship services and our ministries
> phone: 373-4389
> e-mail: central@amaonline.com

Illustration 3b

drama on Saturday night at 7:00 p.m. Illustrations 3a and 3b show two sides of the invitation card.

The following material was what we taught in all of our Sunday morning classes as we strove to reach our mission field with the gospel. The diagram illustrates the format for presenting the class. Begin by breaking the class into small groups for the fellowship time. Next bring the class together so the teacher can present the lesson for the day. Then split into groups again for the final time of prayer, ministry and reflection.

Much of this material was taken from or inspired by material from Ken Houts Care Ministries. I highly recommend his program and material.

Please contact Ken Houts at:

> Care Ministries
> 9412 Delmar
> Prairie Village, KS 66207
> or call 913-381-0242

Dr. Jon Ellas is another excellent trainer in evangelism and small home groups, and also provides churches a comprehensive diagnostic evaluation service.

He can be contacted at:

> Center for Church Growth
> P.O. Box 691006
> Houston, Texas 77269-1006
> (281) 894-4391

70

SUNDAY MORNING ADULT CLASS TOPICS
God's Plan for a Mission-Driven Church

January 3   The Values of a Mission-Driven Church

January 10   We Grow through Personal Relationships and
                 Fellowship

January 17   Relationships within the Body Are Essential

January 24   Ministry Comes through Training and Needs
                 Fulfillment

January 31   Special 5th Sunday Event

February 7   The Value of Leadership and Teamwork

February 14   God Is a Big God and Individual Christians
                 Have Powerful Ministries

February 21   Disciple Making Is for Every Christian

God's Plan for a Mission-Driven Church

Our Goals

1. To change the emphasis of Central from a maintenance-driven church to a mission-driven church.
2. To utilize as many people as possible to reach out to friends and relatives.
3. To have a special outreach day on Easter, April 4.

I. Values defined: Values are the convictions of the way we think things ought to be done. They are those eternal principles we will always want to follow in the church.

II. Four things values do.
   A. They drive us toward our goals.
   B. They define our ministries.
   C. They give purpose and meaning to what we are doing.
   D. They produce a passion in our hearts to fulfill God's plans for us.

III. Overview of the Ten Values
   A. God Is a Big God!
      1. Genesis 1:1
      2. Psalm 50:10-12
      3. Matthew 28:16-20
      4. Colossians 1:23
   B. We Grow through Personal Relationships
      1. Matthew 22:37-38
      2. Research shows most people know twenty people who are unsaved.
   C. Ministry Comes through Needs Fulfillment
      1. Luke 4:18
      2. What are some important needs people have in this community?
   D. Individual Christians Have Powerful Ministries
      1. Ephesians 4:11-13
      2. What does God want you to do?

E. Relationships within the Body Are Essential
   1. John 13:34-35
   2. Ephesians 4:16
F. Fellowship Builds Community
   1. Acts 2:42
   2. Acts 2:46-47
G. Training Is Vital for Growth
   1. Deuteronomy 6:1-9
   2. Ephesians 6:13-18
   3. What training classes would help you?
H. The Value of Leadership by the Members
   1. 1 Peter 4:10-11
   2. How can you use your leadership gifts?
I. Disciple-Making Is for Every Christian
   1. Acts 2:38-47
   2. Write down the name of someone you will pray for beginning today. Do you think they will become a Christian?
J. We Work as a Team
   1. Definition of Team Ministry: Two or more people with a common vision and mutual goals who work together.
   2. Habakkuk 2:2
   3. How do you feel about Central's new emphasis on reaching the lost with the Gospel?

God's Plan for a Mission-Driven Church

Lesson 2 — January 10, 1999
We Grow through Personal Relationships and Fellowship

Breakout before Class: Share your name, where you were born, your best friend growing up, and why you value that friendship.

(Breakout before class: 3 to 10 people in small groups for *Fellowship*.)

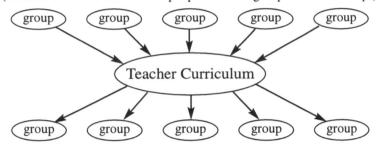

(Breakout after class: small groups to *Pray, Minister, Reflect*.)

I. We Grow through Personal Relationships
   A. Ezekiel 34:1-31
   B. Questions
      1. What were the shepherds doing? (2-3)
      2. Five different groups of sheep are mentioned. What care was needed by each? (4)
      3. What happened to the sheep because of bad shepherds? (5-8)
      4. What will God do to the shepherds for this malpractice? (9-10)
      5. What does God want done for the sheep? (11-16)
      6. After God rounds up the flock, what groups will be found among them? (16-22)
      7. Who will be as a shepherd over them? (23-24)
      8. What will God do to the land on which he pastures his flock with close relationships? (25-31)
   C. Definition of a Relational Church: People we know on a first-name basis who are presently unchurched or unsaved.

      1. Most people know the names of **20** people who are unchurched or unsaved.

      2. Multiply the size of your class by 20 and it will give you the relational size of your class. It is _____.

II. Fellowship Builds Community

  A. Acts 2:42

      1. They had a Habit of __doctrine__.

      2. They had a Habit of __fellowship__.

      3. They had a Habit of __Lord's supper__.

      4. They had a Habit of __prayer__ and __coming__ together.

  B. Definition of Fellowship: Sharing the common life, common faith, common goals, common struggles, common victories.

  C. 7-Role Progression of Fellowship

      1. Fellowship produces __listening__.

      2. Listening produces __understanding__.

      3. Understanding produces __value__.

      4. Value produces __love__.

      5. Love produces __relationship__.

      6. Relationship produces __mission__.
      Love is the bond for our fellowship.

      7. Mission produces or results in __making__ __disciples__.

Breakout after class: Have each person share a personal need, really listen to one another and pray for each other.

God's Plan for a Mission-Driven Church

Breakout before Class: Share the name of one of your friends at Central. Discuss how you made friends at Central.

(Breakout before class: 3 to 10 people in small groups for *Fellowship*.)

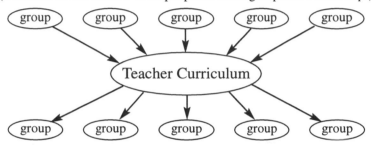

(Breakout after class: small groups to *Pray, Minister, Reflect.*)

I. Relationships Release the Love of God
  A. Threefold Purpose of Relationships (Ezekiel 37:6-7; Ephesians 4:16)
      1. __Fit__ Us Together
      2. __Hold__ Us Together
      3. __Supply__ Our Spiritual Needs
  B. Four Symptoms of Dry Bones
      1. We are spiritually stagnant.
      2. Our "comfort zone" lies in living a life that is less than the life God created us to live (Matthew 14:28).
      3. We are spiritually barren and nonproductive.
      4. We have too many inactive members in church (Ephesians 4:12).
  C. Three Causes of Spiritual Barrenness
      1. We have an attitude problem in regard to people outside the church (I John 4:4).
      2. All of our activities are Christian activities.
      3. Most of our friends are Christians.

D. Statistics Show the Need for Relationships
1. Seventy-five to ninety-five percent of people visit church because of a personal invitation.
2. Seventy-five percent of first-time attendees are looking for relationships.
3. First-time attendees need to make four friends the first month.
4. Follow up is eighty-five percent more effective when done by people who are not paid staff.
5. Ministry recruiting and mobilization occurs primarily through relationships.

Breakout after Class: Put down the names of 20 of your unchurched friends. Share some of them with the the group. Pray for them.

* Homework assignment is to find addresses for the names.

God's Plan for a Mission-Driven Church

Lesson 4 — January 24, 1999
Ministry Comes through Training and Needs Fulfillment

Breakout before Class: Share needs of one another in your group and pray for one another.

(Breakout before class: 3 to 10 people in small groups for *Fellowship*.)

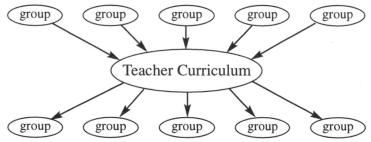

(Breakout after class: small groups to *Pray, Minister, Reflect*.)

I. The Value of Training

    A. Training to be an impact player (Psalm 1:2).

        1. Establish a time to make a daily appointment with God.

        2. Establish a place to meet with God daily.

        3. Establish an agenda regarding what you are going to read and pray about.

        4. Keep a journal of what you talked to God about as well as his answers.

    B. 3 Ways to Develop the Faith to Succeed

        1. Praise Him — it is the doorway (Psalm 100:4).

        2. Pray in the Spirit (Jude 20).

        3. Confess your Faith (2 Corinthians 10:4-5).

    C. Six Steps to Success

        1. Be up and available so God can do a miracle through you.

        2. Get up early for your divine appointments.

        3. Pray up so God will lift you to a higher spiritual realm to serve.

4. Build up your faith to carry out God's plan.
5. Look up for needs. Visitors are miracles disguised as needs.
6. Step up to be God's servant to fulfill these needs.

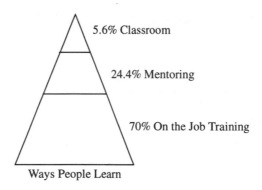

Ways People Learn

D. What training does.
    1. Training produces competence.
    2. Competence produces confidence.
    3. Confidence produces success.
II. The Value of Need Fulfillment Ministry
    A. What was the 5-fold Mission of Jesus in Luke 4:18-19?
    B. Types of Needs
        1. Physical
        2. Relational: marriage, children, work, church.
        3. Psychological: Discouragement, fear, unbelief.
        4. Personal: Pride, profit, pleasure, peace, job, money.
        5. Heartfelt: Accepted, appreciated, belonging, needed.

The Church that meets needs will be the Church that grows.

Breakout after Class: What are some of the needs of the 20 names on your list? Share them and pray in the group for them.

NOTE: Lessons resume with lesson 5 on February 7 after a special 5th Sunday Event on the 31st.

God's Plan for a Mission-Driven Church

Lesson 5 — February 7, 1999
The Value of Leadership and Teamwork

Breakout before Class: What encourages you to attend this class and be in this group?

(Breakout before class: 3 to 10 people in small groups for *Fellowship.*)

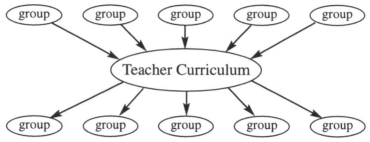

(Breakout after class: small groups to *Pray, Minister, Reflect.*)

I. The Value of Leadership by the Members
  A. The Jesus Training Model
      1. He had a team of 12 men.
      2. He taught them how to minister.
      3. He trained them.
      4. He was a mentor to them.
      5. Together they turned the world upside down.
  B. The Leadership of the 70 and Their Training Model (Luke 10:1-24)
      1. They were well trained.
      2. They knew where to go and what to say.
      3. They knew how to deal with rejection.
      4. They had a clear vision.
      5. When they returned, they were filled with joy and shared stories of success.
      6. Their leader, Jesus, listened to their reports.
      7. Jesus praised their effort.
      8. Jesus praised them because their names were written in heaven.

II. The Value of Team Ministry
  A. Definition of Team Ministry: Two or more people bonded together by a common __vision__ and relating together to achieve a __common__ __goal__.
  B. What did the Lord declare about a people who became a team?
     1. Genesis 11:6
     2. "nothing they purpose to do will be impossible to them."
  C. Team Ministry
     1. Supports through __a common vision__.
     2. Sustains through __common goals__.
     3. Strengthens through __common relationships__.
  D. Servants feel chosen by God to serve on a team. They are deeply influenced by Ephesians 4.
     1. Who: God chose you to be his people (v. 1).
     2. What: Christ gave each one of us a special gift (v. 7).
     3. Why: Christ gave these gifts to prepare God's holy people for the work of serving (v. 12).
     4. When: Each part does its own work (v. 12).
     5. Results: This makes the whole body grow and be filled with love (v. 16).
     6. Message: Say and do what people need to help them become stronger (v. 29).

Breakout after Class: Prioritize your list of twenty names and devise a strategy of how you might get some of them to special events, Easter services, the class, a group or set up a study with them. Discuss this in your groups and pray.

God's Plan for a Mission-Driven Church

Lesson 6 — February 14, 1999
God Is a Big God and Individual Christians Have Powerful Ministries

Breakout before Class: Share a time when someone helped you when you were really down and out.

(Breakout before class: 3 to 10 people in small groups for *Fellowship.*)

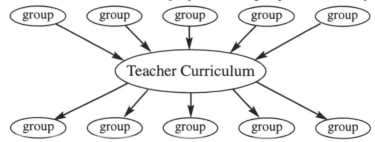

(Breakout after class: small groups to *Pray, Minister, Reflect.*)

I. God Is a Big God
- A. God's Command: Matthew 28:16-20
- B. God's Promise: Philippians 4:19
- C. The Early Church Fulfilled God's Command
    1. The goal was to make disciples (Matthew 28:16-20).
    2. Doubters were overcome (Matthew 28:17).
    3. They had a sense of urgency (Luke 24:46-49; Acts 1:12).
    4. There was tremendous emphasis on prayer (Acts 1:14).
    5. They enlisted additional workers and delegated responsibility (Acts 1:23-26).
    6. Everyone's talents were utilized as workers for the Lord (Acts 2:46-47).
    7. They organized and appointed leaders (Acts 6:1-6).
    8. The multitude was attracted (Acts 2:2).
    9. They were willing to work hard to overcome opposition (Acts 2:12-13).

10. The main objective was saving souls (Acts 2:41).

11. There were steady and continuous opportunities for growth (Acts 8:4).

12. There was great unity in the church (Acts 2:42).

13. They spread the message of Jesus throughout the city (Acts 5:28).

14. They gave God the credit and the praise (Acts 2:47).

15. Personal evangelism was a priority (Acts 5:42).

16. They had outstanding, soul winning teachers (Acts 6:7).

II. Individual Christians Have Powerful Ministries.

    A. 1 Peter 4:10-11

        1. Each person has been given a spiritual gift.

        2. He should use this gift to serve others.

        3. God will provide him strength and wisdom to serve.

        4. He should serve in a way that God will be praised.

    B. Find hurting people with needs and use your God given gifts to help them.

    C. Seven Signs of Hurting People

        1. People's countenances.

        2. People's eyes, which are the window of the soul.

        3. People sitting alone.

        4. People with their heads down.

        5. People new to your section.

        6. People who act tentatively.

        7. People who sit in the back.

    D. Seven Conditions of Hurting People

        1. They are discouraged with their life.

        2. They have no spiritual direction.

        3. They are lonely.

        4. They are weak and vulnerable.

        5. They are wounded.

        6. They feel condemned.

        7. They are spiritually hungry.

    E. (See Involvement/Spiritual Gifts Perspective on the next page.)

Involvement / Spiritual Gifts Perspective

Where your Spiritual Gifts can be used most effectively!

One of the best ways to grow as a Christian is to get involved. Identifying your natural and spiritual motivation will help. Many believers desire personal growth, but seldom find a rewarding ministry.

The following is a summary of sixteen Spiritual Gifts and how they can impact your life. Find the three Spiritual Gifts that best fit you and review what it says about those specific gifts.

SHOWING MERCY

Abilities: Giving sympathy and/or empathy to the hurting.
Opportunities: Hospital, Benevolence, Counseling.
Warning: Don't be a sucker to everyone.
Reward: Knowing you helped those who no one else would help.
Prayer: *"Dear God. Use me to not only help people by showing care, but also sharing truth and TOUGH LOVE when necessary."*

ADMINISTRATION / RULING

Abilities: Organizing or delegating tasks.
Opportunities: Group Leader, Office, Personnel.
Warning: Avoid thinking everyone will get involved.
Reward: Seeing people work together to accomplish difficult tasks.
Prayer: *"Dear God. Help me to be tolerant to those who don't respond like I think they should."*

FAITH

Abilities: Unique ability to trust God and His Word for the impossible.
Opportunities: Prayer, Counseling, Finances.
Warning: Believe, as everything depends upon God, but work, as though everything depends upon you.
Reward: Influencing others to increase their faith.
Prayer: *"Dear God, Increase my faith, while I increase my work for you. Don't let me become lazy."*

PROPHECY

Abilities: Discern right from wrong / Declare truth.
Opportunities: Community / National Concern, Finances, Steering Committee.
Warning: Don't be obnoxious or opinionated.
Reward: Helping others see the truth clearly.
Prayer: *"Dear God, Give me the sensitivity to show love, while sharing truth that may offend."*

APOSTLESHIP

Abilities: Start new churches / Pioneer new works.
Opportunities: Missions, Evangelism, Discipleship.
Warning: Be accountable to others.
Reward: Establishing new ministries that grow.
Prayer: *"Dear God. Keep my eyes on you, not on my vision. For YOU are always more important than what I do for you."*

GIVING

Abilities: Using stewardship to further God's Kingdom.
Opportunities: Finance or Planning Committee, Office.
Warning: Don't use money to control others.
Reward: Knowing you contributed to the advancement of ministry without any personal recognition.
Prayer: *"Dear God. Use my success with finances to bless the ministry and others."*

PASTOR / SHEPHERD

Abilities: Ministering to groups needing leadership.
Opportunities: Committee Chairperson, Visitation.
Warning: Don't get discouraged with those who don't follow.
Reward: Seeing the ministry improve.
Prayer: *"Dear God. Help me be patient with those who are apathetic or spiritually weak."*

DISCERNMENT

Abilities: Special insight concerning good and evil.
Opportunities: Counseling, Prayer, Personnel.
Warning: Guard against quick judgements.
Reward: Protecting others from poor decisions.
Prayer: *"Dear God, Give me a meek and quiet spirit, so that I can share your truth in love and not with pride."*

HOSPITALITY

Abilities: Welcoming people into their home.
Opportunities: Homeless, Encouragement, Housing.
Warning: Balance your family and personal needs with constantly inviting people to your home.
Reward: Giving others a comfortable rest and time of fellowship.
Prayer: *"Dear God. Help me to work as hard at being close to you as I do at being hospitable."*

HELPS / SERVING

Abilities: Serving behind the scenes.
Opportunities: Nursery, Sunday School, Ushering.
Warning: Don't become weary in well doing.
Reward: Knowing you make a difference doing what no one else may want to do.
Prayer: *"Dear God, Thank you for appreciating my labor of love, regardless of what others may fail to appreciate."*

EVANGELISM

Abilities: Comfortably share the gospel with results.
Opportunities: Visitation, Outreach, Missions.
Warning: Don't think everyone should be as dedicated to evangelism as you are.
Reward: Leading people to Christ glorifies God.
Prayer: *"Dear God, Increase my vision for the lost, while helping me to understand why others do not share my burden."*

KNOWLEDGE

Abilities: Special ability to remember many things, especially from the Bible.
Opportunities: Counseling, Book Store, Library.
Warning: Don't get puffed up with much knowledge.
Reward: Helping others learn things they never knew.
Prayer: *"Dear God, You are the all-knowing One. May I only know and share what you want me to. Also help me not to be proud of my knowledge"*

TEACHING

Abilities: Clarify truth / Insights as to why facts are true.
Opportunities: Teaching, Training, Library.
Warning: Don't neglect other responsibilities.
Reward: Knowing people learn the truth.
Prayer: *"Dear God, Help me to be practical, not just impart truth."*

EXHORTATION

Abilities: Share practical steps of action.
Opportunities: Counseling, Crisis Center, Evangelism.
Warning: Choose words wisely.
Reward: Seeing people respond to your advice and helping them through problems.
Prayer: *"Dear God, Use me to say what you would have me to say, not what I feel at the moment."*

LEADERSHIP

Abilities: Obvious influence to motivate others.
Opportunities: Men's or Women's Ministries, Discipleship, Support Groups.
Warning: Lead by example, not just motivation.
Reward: Developing leaders to take over what you have done.
Prayer: *"Dear God, Make me a strong and sensitive leader. Help me to be a well-balanced leader!"*

WISDOM

Abilities: Special insights to make wise decisions.
Opportunities: Prayer, Counseling, Finances.
Warning: Don't become proud of your wisdom.
Reward: Helping others make good decisions.
Prayer: *"Dear God, May my wisdom always come from you and not my own judgement. Help me to always rely on your Word and not my opinions."*

Used by permission

Breakout after Class: Identify what you think is one of your gifts from the spiritual gifts page. Discuss your strengths and weaknesses in ministering to these hurting people. Pray for one another.

God's Plan for a Mission-Driven Church

Lesson 7 — February 21, 1999
Disciple-making Is for Every Christian

Breakout before Class: Share your story in your own words of why you became a Christian or why you are searching if you are not a Christian.

(Breakout before class: 3 to 10 people in small groups for *Fellowship*.)

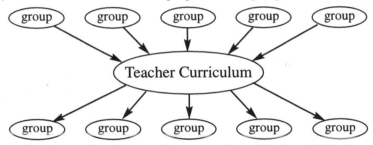

(Breakout after class: small groups to *Pray, Minister, Reflect.*)

I. Three Keys of Ministering to Hurting People
- A. Ministry must be *personal*.
- B. Ministry must meet *needs*.
- C. Ministry must be *relational*.

II. Five Levels of Communication
- A. "Cliché Level"
- B. "Fact Level"
- C. "Opinion Level"
- D. "Emotion and Feeling Level"
- E. "Peak Experience Level"

III. The A.I.D. Communication System (This helps you begin a conversation, keep it on track, discover a person's needs and establish a relationship with someone you do not know.)
- A. **A**pproach Step reminds you to become a *visitor's friend.* Ask questions about things that are important to them.
- B. **I**nterview Step is a time to *discover their needs.*
- C. **D**emonstration Step is where we demonstrate our love for the visitor and show our *desire to meet their needs.*

IV. The I.E.N. Principle also helps us get better acquainted with visitors.

A. **I** stands for *interest.* Find what their major interests are.

B. **E** stands for *entertainment.* Ask them what they do for entertainment.

C. **N** stands for *needs.* After you have found out their interests and what entertainment they enjoy, you should not have much trouble finding out their needs.

V. We are trying to lead these people to become disciples.

A. **Initated into** — Personal faith in Jesus Christ (Acts 2:38).

B. **Integrated** — Involved in, or functioning as part of the local church (Acts 2:42).

C. **Disciple** — Knows the vision, values, and biblical truths followed by the local church and is following the Lord Jesus Christ (Acts 5:42).

VI. **Stages Involved in the Spiritual Development of Disciples***

	DISCIPLER			DISCIPLE		
	Discipler's Role	Discipler's Tasks	Discipler's Responsibility	Disciple's Responsibility	Disciple's Commitment	Disciple's Development
Stage 1	Witness (1 Cor 1:18; 2:1-5)	Evangelism	(Scale of 1-10) 10 (greatest) 9	(Scale of 1-10) 1 (least) 2	*Friendship* that leads to claiming Christ's *Lordship*	From *unbeliever* to *spiritual babe*
Stage 2	Parent (1 Cor 3:1-3)	Follow-up	8 7	3 4	Claiming Christ's *Lordship* that leads to *discipleship*	From *spiritual babe* to spiritual disciple
Stage 3	Servant (1 Cor 3:5-6)	Training	6 5	5 6	*Discipleship* that leads to leadership	From *spiritual disciple* to multiplying leader
Stage 4	Steward (1 Cor 4:1; 3:10-16)	Equipping	4 3	7 8	*Leadership* that leads to partnership	From *multiplying leader* to colaborer
Stage 5	Encourager (1 Cor 3:7-9; 4:16,17)	Supporting	2 1 (least)	9 10 (greatest)	*Partnership* that leads to churchmanship	From *colaborer* to discipler

Breakout after Class: Share some ways to invite people to class, services, or special events. Pray for God to bless you as you invite the people on your list.

*Permission granted by 1988 Broadman & Holman Bible Publishers, Life Helps Division.

SIX WEEKS OF NEW LIFE

February 28   "God Has the World Ready for the Gospel of
               Christ"

March 7   "The Early Church Was a Mission-Driven
               Church"

March 14   "What Makes People Receptive to the
               Gospel"

March 21   "The Importance of Sharing the Gospel"

March 28   "A Love Message for Reaching Your Friends"

April 4   "Easter Harvest"

Six Weeks of New Life

Lesson 1 — February 28
"God Has the World Ready for the Gospel of Christ"

Goal: Partner with the class to become a team on a six-weeks' mission trip in Amarillo. The climax will be our Easter Services and class on April 4 as we pray for a great Harvest of Souls.

Pray: For a great Harvest of Souls

Action Steps:
1. Set outreach goals in class.
2. Strive to contact, invite and teach the twenty names on your mission field card.
3. Pray for one another and the people we are inviting.
4. Encourage one another in fellowship.
5. Catch the vision as we make disciples for Christ.
6. Work as a spiritual team.

I. God Had the World Ready for Jesus Christ Nearly 2,000 Years Ago

> Theme verse: "When the fullness of time had come,
> God sent forth his Son" Galatians 4:4.

A. His birth in Bethlehem prophesied.
1. Matthew 2:3-6 Herod asked the religious leaders where Christ was to be born.
a. They quoted Micah's prophecy (Micah 5:2) given 700 years earlier naming Bethlehem as the place Jesus would be born.
b. Isaiah 7:14 also quoted hundreds of years earlier about the virgin birth of Jesus.

B. Childhood of Christ
1. Luke 2:40 "child became strong; he was filled with wisdom and the grace of God was upon him."
2. Luke 2:41-43
a. Amazed rabbis with his questions and answers.
b. Conscious of his unique relationship with God.
c. Fully aware of his unique mission.

C. Greek Language and Culture
1. Acts 21:37 Roman captain asked Paul, "Can you speak Greek?"

2. From 336 to 323 BC, Alexander the Great conquered Persia, Egypt and the Middle Eastern World, spreading the Greek language to all conquered areas. In the providence of God, this provided an almost universal language that would carry the Gospel of Christ throughout the Mediterranean World.

3. The New Testament was written in Greek, the international language of the day.
   a. The Old Testament was written in Hebrew — a language of one people.
   b. The Greek language of the New Testament fit God's purpose to form the church out of believers of all kindreds, nations, and peoples. (Acts 2:4-12)
   c. Many Greeks had lost faith in their pagan gods and were beginning to open up to a real faith that would answer their questions about life (Acts 17:15-34).

4. The Rule of Augustus Caeser from 31 B.C.–A.D. 14 brought a brief time of peace unparalleled in history. It was called the Pax Romana. It allowed the first missionaries to travel safely throughout the world.

5. The Jewish world and religions composed of Pharisees, Sadducees, and Herodians became very divided and were searching for something better.

II. God Has the World Ready for Christ As We Approach the Year 2,000.
   A. World WWJD Movement (What Would Jesus Do?)
   B. World "Call to Be Servants" Movement
   C. Primarily Peace in World
   D. Fall of Iron Curtain and Berlin Wall (Many new countries receptive to the gospel.)
   E. Technology in travel and communication.
   F. World movement of Jews for Christ turning to the gospel.
   G. Emergence of the U.S. as the only world power.
   H. Moral and religious decline of the U.S. There are now more missionaries sent to the U.S. from other countries than there are missionaries sent from the U.S. to other countries.
   I. Receptivity of People in the U.S. to Seek God and Come to Church
      1. 40% of all people are changing religions seeking God.

2. 20% of all people move each year and 50% are changing religions seeking God.
3. Millions of people in the U.S. are attending church for the first time. However, 50% of the Baby Boomers who did not grow up attending church had not attended a single church service as of 1990 and 85% of the Baby Busters had never attended a single church service. Boomers are those born 1947-1965. Busters are those born after 1965.

J. The Year 2,000
K. The Economy

Discussion: Do you think Amarillo is receptive to the gospel? What can you do to get the twenty on your mission field list to church Easter. What can all of us do to reach them?

Six Weeks of New Life

Lesson 2 — March 7
"The Early Church Was a Mission-Driven Church"

Purpose: Learn from the early church and work as a class team to teach those on our list.

Message: Focus our prayer and outreach efforts on those in need of help.

Action Steps:
    1. Pray about the twenty on my list.
    2. Invite friends for Easter.

Key Scripture: Enlarge the place of your tent,
            stretch your tent curtains wide,
            do not hold back;
        lengthen your cords,
            strengthen your stakes (Isaiah 54:2).

  I. Consider and list the people in the following groups who are within an hour driving distance from the church.

    A. **Common Kinship** — People related biologically or through marriage (immediate family, aunts, uncles, in-laws, nieces, nephews, grandparents, etc.).

      1. _____   6. _____
      2. _____   7. _____
      3. _____   8. _____
      4. _____   9. _____
      5. _____ 10. _____

    B. **Common Friendship** — People you know on a first name basis (friends, from work, neighbors).

      1. _____   6. _____
      2. _____   7. _____
      3. _____   8. _____
      4. _____   9. _____
      5. _____ 10. _____

    C. **Common Associates** — People you associate with at grocery stores, cleaners, beauty salon, workplace, etc.

      1. _____   6. _____

2. _____	7. _____
3. _____	8. _____
4. _____	9. _____
5. _____	10. _____

II. What or who was responsible for leading you to Christ and the church?

Special Need	1-2%
Walk-In	2-3%
Minister	5-6%
Visitation	1-2%
Sunday School/Small Group	4-5%
Evangelistic Crusade or Gospel Meeting	½ of 1%
Church Outreach Program	2-3%
Friend or Relative	75-90%

III. The Early Church Was a Mission-Driven Church. The church reached out in Jerusalem and Israel through:

A. Commissioning — Jesus gave them the commandment to evangelize in Jerusalem, Samaria and among all nations: Acts 1:8.

B. Praying — continued in prayer in the upper room: Acts. 1:14.

C. Empowerment — On the day of Pentecost, the Holy Spirit came upon the Upper Room congregation of 120 people and filled them with power to teach the gospel and evangelize. They shared their faith with the masses and there were 3,000 conversions: Acts 2:1-44.

D. Witnessing — They taught, suffered persecution, united in prayer, shared their faith and worldly goods and rejoiced they were counted worthy to suffer for his name: Acts 3–5.

E. Serving — The first "deacons" were chosen and were commissioned to serve tables: Acts 6.

F. Martyrdom — Stephen was the first Christian martyred for preaching the gospel: Acts 7.

G. Persecution and Scattering — As they went, they evangelized, winning souls to Christ. Philip, the first evangelist, conducted a soul-winning evangelistic crusade: Acts 8–9.

Discussion: How many will this class invite to church for Easter? How many do you think will come?

Six Weeks of New Life

Lesson 3 — March 14
"What Makes People Receptive to the Gospel"

Purpose: Learn how stress and needs make people more receptive to the Gospel.

Message: Provide God's message and His love extended through you to meet the needs of the unchurched.

Action Steps:
1. Understand the receptivity principles.
2. Focus on the needs of your prospects.
3. Pray for your prospects.
4. See how God's word and spiritual principles can address the needs of the unchurched.

Key Statement: The higher the stress factor, the more receptive the person is to the gospel.

Key Verse: "I became all things to all men that I might by all means save some." 1 Corinthians 9:22

Take the stress test: Score _____

Look over the list and meditate on the stress of your prospects.

100	Death of Spouse
73	Divorce
65	Marital Separation
63	Jail Term
63	Death of a Close Family Member
53	Personal Injury or Illness
50	Marriage
47	Fired from Work
46	Marital Reconciliation
45	Retirement
44	Change in Family Member's Health
40	Pregnancy
39	Sex Difficulties
39	Addition to Family
39	Business Readjustment
38	Change in Financial Status
37	Death of a Close Friend
35	Change in Number of Marital Arguments
31	Mortgage or Loan over $10,000
30	Foreclosure

Steps in Responding to Stress and Problems

1. We admit that we are powerless over our problems if we try to handle them alone.
   (Job 6:2-13) "I am utterly helpless, without any hope" LB.

2. We believe that God can help us.
   (Job 19:25-27) "I know that my Redeemer lives."

3. We will turn our life over to the care of God.
   (Psalm 61:1-8) "I will cry to you for help. . . . lead me to the . . . Rock of safety. . . . You are my refuge" LB.

4. We will search and make a moral inventory of ourselves.
   (Nehemiah 9:1-3) "The laws of God were read aloud to them for two or three hours, and for several more hours they took turns confessing their own sins" LB.

5. We admit the exact nature of our wrongs.
   (Genesis 38:1-30) "Judah admitted that they were his and said, 'She is more in the right than I am'" LB.

6. We are ready for God to remove our defects of character.
   (Psalm 51:7-19) "Wash me and I shall be whiter than snow. . . .

Create in me a new, clean heart, O God, filled with clean thoughts and right desires" LB.

7. We humbly ask God to remove our past problems.
   (Jeremiah 18:1-6) "The jar that he was forming didn't turn out as he wished, so he kneaded it into a lump and started again. . . . As the clay is in the potter's hand, so are you in my hand" LB.

8. We will make a list of people we have hurt.
   (James 5:16) "Admit your faults to one another and pray for each other so that you may be healed" LB.

9. We will try to make things right with people we have wronged.
   (Psalm 37:21) "Evil men borrow and 'cannot pay it back'! But the good man returns what he owes with some extra besides" LB.

10. We will continue to take daily inventory of our lives and promptly admit our mistakes.
    (Ephesians 4:26) "If you are angry, don't sin by nursing your grudge. Don't let the sun go down with you still angry" LB.

11. We will seek God's way through study, prayer, and meditation.
    (Psalm 27:1-6) "The one thing I want from God . . . is the privilege of meditating in his Temple, living in his presence every day of my life . . . . There I'll be when trouble comes. . . . He will set me on a high rock out of reach of all my enemies" LB.

12. Because of God's grace to us, we will carry His message of hope and salvation to others.
    (Mark 16:15-16) "You are to go into all the world and preach the Good News to everyone, everywhere. Those who believe and are baptized will be saved" LB.

Discussion: Share how adversity or stress brought you closer to God or led to the salvation of someone you know.

Six Weeks of New Life

Lesson 4 — March 21
"The Importance of Sharing the Gospel"

Purpose: Develop a strategy for you to invite those people on your
mission field card to come to Easter services.

Message: Do our spiritual homework so the unchurched are receptive to the gospel.

Action Steps:

1. Each person put down his individual goal for the number of people he will invite to Easter services and the number he believes will come.
2. Have the class put down the total number who will be invited and the number they believe will come.
3. Pray for those on your list and for this Easter special event.
4. Follow the steps in inviting your friends to come.

I. Invitational Steps

   A. Pray for each person on your list.

   B. Be with each person on your list prior to the invitation. Have a pleasant contact with them, ask questions and let them do 80% of the talking.

   C. Send them some printed material from the church about the Easter service.

   D. Give each person a personal, verbal invitation.

   E. Offer to come by and pick them up.

   F. Give them a reminder call Saturday night.

II. The Importance of Sharing the Gospel

Key Verse: "Everyone who calls on the name of the Lord will be saved"
Romans 10:13.

   A. First Question: "How can they call on the one they have not believed in?" (Romans 10:14)
The Answer: The lost cannot call on the Lord to be saved until they believe:

      1. "That Christ died for our sins" (1 Corinthians 15:3).

      2. "That he was buried" (1 Corinthians 15:4).

      3. "That he was raised on the third day according to the Scriptures" (1 Corinthians 15:4).

B. Second Question: "How can they believe in the one of whom they have not heard?" (Romans 10:14)
   The Answer: The lost cannot believe in Him until they hear the good news of salvation.
   1. The eunuch had to hear to believe (Acts 8:26:39).
   2. Paul had to hear to believe (Acts 9:1-8).
   3. Cornelius had to hear to believe (Acts 10:1-48).
   4. The Philippian jailer had to hear to believe (Acts 16:25-40).
C. Third Question: "How can they hear without someone teaching or preaching to them?" (Romans 10:14)
   The Answer: They cannot hear the good news of salvation without someone sharing the gospel with them.
   1. Three thousand were taught, repented, were baptized, and became new converts at Pentecost because they were taught the gospel (Acts 2:14-40).
   2. The eunuch was taught and baptized by Philip (Acts 8:26-39).
   3. Paul became a Christian because Stephen (Acts 7:54-60), Jesus (Acts 9:1-10), and Ananias (Acts 9:11-18) all witnessed and taught him.
   4. Cornelius and his household were saved because Peter taught them (Act 10:1-48).
   5. The Philippian jailer believed and was baptized because Paul and Silas taught him (Acts 16:25-40).
   6. You became a Christian because someone taught you.

Discussion: Who taught you the gospel? Who is going to lead the people on your mission field list to Christ?

Six Weeks of New Life

Lesson 5 — March 28
"A Love Message for Reaching Your Friend"

Purpose: To implement our class training by getting our friends to next Sunday's Easter Service. To use this event as a step to later lead them to Jesus Christ.

Message: We have a specific responsibility, we have caught the vision, and we have set some specific individual and class goals.

Decision: Determine all we will do to reach our "unchurched" friends.

Proclaim: The "Good News" of Jesus Christ and God's love for the "unchurched."

Key Verse: "A man's heart plans his way, But the LORD directs his steps" (Proverbs 16:9, NKJV).

I. Objectives of This Plan
   A. Personal Relationships (Earn the right to share the gospel.)
   B. Involvement with Other Christians (People need five or six exposures to the gospel before they usually make a commitment.)
   C. Multiple Exposures to the Gospel (People need to know the kind of people who are in the church.)
   D. Spending Time with People (Most people spend more time in planning vacations than planning how to minister to their friends.)
   E. Include Prayer and God in Your Planning
   F. Be a Servant-Driven Missionary and Fulfill Your Goals

II. Five Bonds of Love (Colossians 3:14)
   A. Bond of Unconditional Love
      1. Accept the person as they are.
      2. Unconditional love frees us from two terrible fears.
         a. Fear of failure.
         b. Fear of rejection.
      3. Proverbs 24:16 "For a righteous man may fall seven times and rise again" NKJV.
   B. Bond of Affirmation
      1. See the good in a person and tell them about it.

2. Proverbs 15:30 "A good report makes the bones healthy" NKJV.
3. Psychologists tell us people need fourteen hugs a day.
4. We have an "Appreciation Bucket" in our soul. When we don't receive appreciation, we feel used and empty.

C. Bond of Peace
1. People need friends to make deposits of love in them.
2. Galatians 5:22-23

D. Bond of Serving
1. Serving is love in action. Look for ways to act out love.
2. 1 John 3:16

E. Bond of Forgiving
1. Don't let the sun go down on your anger.
2. 1 Peter 4:8 — "love covers over a multitude of sins."

III. Four Principles of Biblical Love
A. Love grows the more we know people.
(Philippians 1:9 "And this I pray, that your love may abound still more and more in knowledge and all discernment" NKJV.)

B. God's love has been poured into our hearts.
(Romans 5:8 "But God demonstrates His own love toward us, in that while we were still sinners, Christ died for us" NKJV.)

C. Love is very useful during adversity.
(Proverbs 17:17 "A friend loves at all times, and a brother is born for adversity" NKJV.)

D. Love always gives your best.
(1 John 3:16 "By this we know love, because he laid down His life for us. And we also ought to lay down our lives for the brethren" NKJV.)

Discussion: Fill your "Appreciation Buckets" up as you share some words of affirmation with one another.

Close with Prayer: FOR GOD TO PROVIDE A GREAT VICTORY NEXT SUNDAY

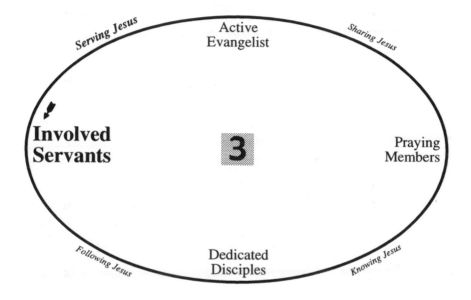

Serving Jesus

Active
Evangelist

Sharing Jesus

Involved
Servants

3

Praying
Members

Following Jesus

Dedicated
Disciples

Knowing Jesus

We're halfway around the race track. For the first quarter, we stressed the importance of **Praying Members** knowing Jesus. We then followed the biblical model from the book of Acts as these Praying Members became **Active Evangelists** sharing Jesus. This model should bring tremendous spiritual and numerical growth to the local church. Now, we are ready for these people for the third quarter to become **Involved Servants** serving Jesus. They need to use their gifts for the glory of God. Members using their gifts will build up His local church.

Prayer and Church Leadership

Prayer is the single greatest responsibility and privilege for church leaders. Just as no church can grow beyond the level of its church leaders, no person can grow spiritually beyond his prayer life. An interesting chart compares a church leader's time spent in prayer each week with his spiritual growth, family life, church development, stewardship, Bible study, evangelism, relationships with others, shepherding, physical health, time management and stress. For simplicity, chart this a week or a month at a time.

	Jan	Feb	Mar	Apr	May	Jun
1. Prayer time						
2. Spiritual growth						
3. Church development						
4. Stewardship						
5. Bible study						
6. Evangelism						
7. Relationships						
8. Shepherding						
9. Physical health						
10. Stress						

• Write in an "H" for "High," "A" for "Average," and "L" for "Low" by each topic per month.

A spiritual exercise for you: If you had to guess, how do you think your "report card" would look? Now try it for a while and see.

This spiritual report card usually reveals much about the importance of prayer in a church leader's life.

Every church leader should have a prayer partner. Prayer provides wisdom and direction. It bonds leaders together. It makes God a partner and close confidant in all situations. Every minister needs to have an elder or deacon who will give him a call and offer to come by and pray with him on a regular basis.

Church leaders need to begin all their meetings with a season of prayer. It's amazing how much more is accomplished in a much shorter time when this is done. These meetings are great times to invite people so you can pray with them and encourage them. You can invite engaged couples who are planning their wedding, couples having a wedding anniversary, widows who have lost their husband, people with special struggles and needs. These meetings should be so filled with prayer that we will destroy the concept of lengthy meetings to micromanage the church!

> Church leaders need to begin all their meetings with a season of prayer.

Consider this: What percentage of the time your church leaders are meeting together is spent in prayer?

Church leaders praying together build teams. They laugh and cry together. They will fight Satan with everything they have if Satan tries to reach one of the team. The burden and time needed is not too great because these church leaders are brothers and sisters in the family of God. They level with one another and never talk behind each others' backs. They care enough about each other to hold themselves accountable to one another. They allow each person to be different using their unique God-given gifts. They constantly affirm one another, and they enjoy being with one another.

It's a high calling to be a church leader, and time management is very important. There are six major time wasters for church leaders.

1. Interruptions (telephone calls, drop-in visitors, distractions)
2. Tasks left unfinished (jumping from one thing to another)
3. Routine tasks involving too much trivia, red tape, and paper work.
4. Attempts to do too much at once (unrealistic time estimates)
5. Personal disorganization

6. Not praying for God to help you better manage your time.

Never forget the importance of your individually pouring your heart out to God. One man has a 15-minute prayer ritual every morning. He first stretches his hands out and thanks God for all the ways he has been blessed in the last 24 hours. He then refers to his daily calendar and asks God to help him prioritize his tasks, and then he asks God's help in accomplishing them. Now he lies face down of the floor and talks to God about his fears and concerns. He imagines himself lying in the palm of God's hand. As each fear is iden-tified, he imagines it running out through his hands into the hand of God! Now, he is ready to face the world and be God's pray-ing servant today!

> Prayer is accepting servanthood instead of pushing my way to the top.

Church Leaders need to al-ways remember that Matthew 7:7 says "Ask and it will be given to you." What a promise! There are also seven don'ts in this one chapter.

Don't:
1. Pick on people with a critical spirit.
2. Be flippant with the sacred.
3. Bargain with God (do what HE wants done).
4. Look for shortcuts to God.
5. Fall for easy answers to complex problems.
6. Impress people by saying only the accepted words.
7. Be impressed with charisma instead of character.

Do: Pray for people. The highest form of a lack of integrity is for church leaders and members to talk behind people's backs.

Matthew 18:15 tells us, "If your brother sins against you, go and show him his fault, just between the two of you." When you place the names of prospective elders or deacons before the congregation, be sure you ask the people to talk to them personally if they have any problem with their serving. If you don't follow this biblical principle, you can create a nightmare for the church. If you ask the people to talk to the elders or someone else, this important principle is violated. Ira North, whom God used to build a congregation of 6,000 members in Madison, Tennessee, used to say that it was impossible to build a large congregation without following Matthew 18:15!

Before congregations can have Involved Servants following Jesus to accomplish his plans for the local church, leaders need to spend quality time with a Church Planning Model.

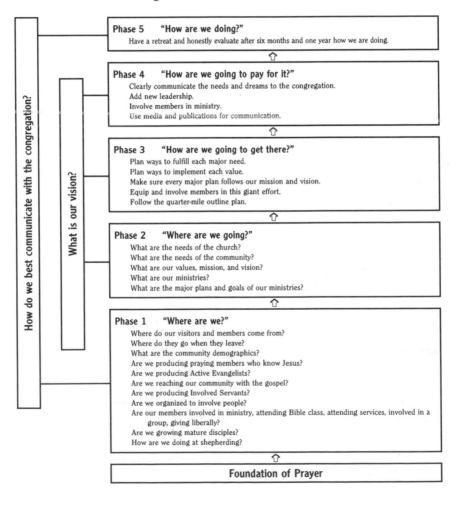

This instrument should be of tremendous value for churches looking for direction in the third millennium. There needs to be two-way communication, openness and vulnerability, teamwork, no hidden agendas, and an overwhelming desire for the church to be all God wants it to be. I pray that church leaders will use this planning tool often because it will be a tremendous help for the local church.

> There needs to be two-way communication, openness and vulnerability.

If you desire more material in this area, let me encourage you to purchase the book entitled *Measuring Church Growth* by Dr. John Ellas. The book is a research-based tool for evaluating and planning. John's address is :

> Center for Church Growth
> P.O. Box 691006
> Houston, Texas, 772169-1006
> Phone: 281-894-4391

When answers to the church planning model are in place, we are ready to build the structure to fulfill these goals and involve people. We had an elders and deacons retreat in October of 1998 where we talked about restructuring our organization which we call the ministry system. We planned to do this some six months later when we would be adding additional elders and deacons. We wanted everything to be bathed in prayer for this gigantic task, so we prepared a devotional guide for the congregation entitled "55 Days of Prayer" We launched the effort on April, 11, 1999. The complete schedule and excerpts of the devotional guide can be found on the following pages (illustrations 4a-4f).

Ask yourself: Are prayer and future planning integral parts of leader selection in your congregation?

Not only did we want our church family praying for 55 days, we also wanted the congregation to be vitally involved in the nomination process. We printed detailed nomination brochures for each member of the congregation. The brochures described the roles and responsibilities of elders and deacons. It gave specific instructions about the nominations process. It listed what

107

Importance of Prayer in Choosing Leaders

Day 1 *April 12*
Then they prayed, "Lord, you know everyone's heart. Show us which of these two you have chosen to take over this apostolic ministry." Acts 1:24
Pray for spiritual wisdom as we nominate leaders.

Day 2 *April 13*
"They devoted themselves to the apostle's teaching and to the fellowship, to the breaking of bread and to prayer." Acts 2:42
Pray for men who love to pray.

Day 3 *April 14*
"After they prayed, the place where they were meeting was shaken." Acts 4:31
Pray for men who understand the power of prayer.

Day 4 *April 15*
"We will give our attention to prayer and the ministry of the word." Acts 6:4
Pray for men who pray and study daily.

Day 5 *April 16*
"Come near to God and he will come near to you." James 4:8
Pray for men who are regularly drawing near to God.

Day 6 *April 17*
"Paul and Barnabas appointed elders for them in each church and, with prayer and fasting, committed them to the Lord, in whom they had put their trust." Acts 14:23
Pray for men whose prayer life demonstrates their great faith.

Central Church of Christ
"An Exciting Place to Call Home"
1401 S. Monroe - Amarillo, TX 79101-4043
(806)373-4389

Elders and Deacons Selection Schedule
55 Days of Prayer

April 11 "Importance of Prayer in Choosing Leaders" Prayer guides handed out to the congregation.

April 18 "Qualifications of Leaders" - Elders and deacons nominating brochure ready. Elders and deacons nominated by the congregation.

April 25 "Servant Leaders" - Elders and deacons nominated by the congregation.

May 2 "Spiritual Leaders" - Prayer and contact with prospective elders and deacons.

May 9 "The Mother and Wife Influence" - Prayer and contact with prospective elders and deacons.

May 16 "Mentors and Examples" - Prayer and contact with prospective elders and deacons.

May 23 "Our Values, Mission and Purpose" - Prospective elders and deacons names before the congregation.

May 30 "Equippers" - Prospective elders and deacons names before the congregation.

June 6 "Honor to Whom Honor is Due" - Elders and deacons installed and deacons orientation.

Servant Leaders

	Servility (Honor Me)	Servanthood (Honor God)
Service is done out of a sense of	obligation	obedience
Priorities are established by a	me-first mindset	Father-first mindset
Motivated to serve by	fear of men	fellowship with God
Attitude reflects	not my job	whatever it takes
Approaches ministry out of	fullness which becomes emptiness	emptiness which becomes fullness
Results are	self-seeking	God-glorifying
A spirit of	pride	humility

Day 14 *April 25* — "The greatest among you will be your servant." Jn 23:11
Pray for a harvest of great servants.

Day 15 *April 26* — "Jesus poured water into a basin and began to wash his disciples' feet, drying them with the towel that was wrapped around him." Jn 13:5
Pray for us to follow this servant example.

Day 16 *April 27* — "No servant is greater than his master nor is a messenger greater than the one who sent him. Jn. 13:16
Pray for us to to have this servant example.

Day 17 *April 28* — "The son of man did not come to be served, but to serve." Matt. 20:28
Pray for leaders who really want to serve.

Qualifications of Leaders

Day 7 *April 18* — Elders - "If anyone sets his heart on being an overseer, he desires a noble task." I Tim. 3:4
Deacons - "Deacons, likewise, are to be men worthy of respect." I Tim. 3:8
Pray for men who meet these qualifications.

Day 8 *April 19* — Elders - "The overseer must be above reproach, the husband of but one wife, temperate, self-controlled." I Tim. 3:2
Deacons - "Deacons must be sincere, not indulging in much wine, and not pursuing dishonest gain." I Tim. 3:8
Pray by name for a potential elder who has these qualifications.

Day 9 *April 20* — Elders - "The overseer must be respectable, hospitable and able to teach." I Tim. 3:2
Deacons - "They must keep hold of the deep truths of the faith with a clear conscience." I Tim. 3:9
Pray by name for a potential deacon who has these qualifications.

Day 10 *April 21* — Elders - "He must not be given to drunkenness, not violent, but gentle, not quarrelsome, not a lover of money." I Tim. 3:3
Deacons - "They must first be tested; and then if there is nothing against them, let them serve as deacons." I Tim. 3:10
Pray for members to nominate people who meet these qualifications.

CENTRAL CHURCH OF CHRIST

1401 S. Monroe
Amarillo, Texas 79101
(806) 373-4389

NINE SHEPHERDS

Rusty Burns
Bob Crass
Ron Freeman
Bill Johnson
John Noyes
Steve Rogers
Shelby Stapleton
Warlick Thomas
Leon Wood

Day 18 *April 29*
"Serve one another in love." Gal. 5:13
Pray for leaders who love to help this church family.

Day 19 *April 30*
"And whatever you do, whether in word or deed, do it all in the name of the Lord Jesus, giving thanks to God the Father though him. Col. 3:17
Pray for leaders who love to praise Jesus.

Day 20 *May 1*
"If anyone serves, he should do it with the strength God provides, so that in all things God may be praised through Jesus Christ." 1 Pet. 4:11
Pray for leaders who serve with all the strength God provides.

Spiritual Leaders

Day 21 *May 2*
"The Lord has sought out a man after his own heart and appointed him leader of his people." 1 Sam. 13:14
Pray for leaders after God's own heart.

Day 22 *May 3*
"I looked for a man among them who would build up the wall and stand before me in the gap on behalf of the land so I would not have to destroy it."
Ezek. 22:30
Pray for leaders who will "stand in the gap" for us.

Day 23 *May 4*
"Humble yourselves, therefore, under God's mighty hand, that he may lift you up in due time." 1 Pet. 5:6
Pray for humble servants

we expected from church leaders and what was provided for them. A thumbnail sketch of the ministries was presented, and members were encouraged to nominate people to serve in specific ministries. A biblical plan to involve every member was in the brochure as well as a diagram of the ministry system. There was also a list of present elders and deacons. Detailed information about The Ministry System can be obtained from a book which I wrote in 1997, *The Servant-Driven Church*. It can be obtained from College Press or your local book store. Appendix B of that book reproduces the 1991 Deacon Nomination Form. The 1999 form used for both deacons and elders is reproduced in illustration 5 of this book.

Many people have also asked about an affirmation of elders form. We use the type of form reproduced in illustration 6 and have had an incredible response from the congregation. We have found it useful to include photographs of the men being affirmed for the sake of those who know them by sight but not by name.

> Prayer is confidence in God's faithfulness to me on an uncharted course toward an unknown future.

Although the forms are not to be signed, we do ask the responders to give some information about themselves on the form.

We had a tremendous installation service on Sunday morning. We had our four new elders share briefly their dream for the Central Church. We had the leaders and their families come forward, lay hands on them, and pray for them. We read the verses to them from the song "Rise Up O Men of God." Teens placed a special servant name tag on the church leaders which they wore throughout the day.

Following the service we had a meal for the deacons, elders, ministers, and their families. Then we had a brief orientation session and each church leader was

Ponder: Are your deacons and elders simply expected to start serving "cold turkey"?

THEY SMELL LIKE **S**HEEP

WHAT THE BIBLE SAYS
SHEPHERDS DO FOR FLOCKS . . .

* **GUARD THE FLOCK** — Acts 20:28
* **WATCH THE FLOCK**
* **FEED THE FLOCK**

* **EQUIP THE FLOCK FOR MINISTRY** — Eph. 4:10-12

* **CARE FOR THE FLOCK** — 1 Tim. 3:5
* **DIRECT THE AFFAIRS OF THE FLOCK**
* **PREACH THE WORD**
* **TEACH THE FLOCK**

* **ENCOURAGE THE FLOCK** — Titus 1:9-10
* **REFUTE FALSEHOOD**

* **PRAY FOR THE FLOCK** — Jas. 1:14
* **ANOINT THE SICK**

* **SERVE THE FLOCK** — 1 Pet. 5:1-5
* **LEAD THE FLOCK**
* **BE AN EXAMPLE TO THE FLOCK**

* **LOSE SLEEP OVER THE FLOCK** — Heb. 13:17

Paul's Five Priorities for the Elders in Acts 20:28-35

a. To keep right with God.
   Keep watch over yourselves and

b. To feed and lead the flock.
   all the flock *of which the Holy Spirit has made you overseers. Be shepherds of the church of God,* which he bought with his own blood.

c. To warn and watch . . . to protect the flock (from false teachers and other emissaries of Satan). I know that *after I leave, savage wolves will come in among you and will not spare the flock.* Even from your own number men will arise and distort the truth in order to draw away disciples after them. So be on your guard! Remember that for three years I never stopped warning each of you night and day with tears.

d. To pray and study.
   Now *I commit you to God and to the word of his grace,* which can build you up and give you an inheritance among all those who are sanctified.

e. To be free from self-interest.
   I have not coveted anyone's silver or gold or clothing. You yourselves know that these hands of mine have supplied my own needs and the needs of my companions. In everything I did, I showed you that by this kind of hard work we must help the weak, remembering the words the Lord Jesus himself said; 'It is more blessed to give than to receive.'

CHRIST

ELDERS

Here is a trustworthy saying: If anyone sets his heart on being an overseer, he desires a noble task. Now the overseer must be above reproach, the husband of but one wife, temperate, self-controlled, respectable, hospitable, able to teach, not given to drunkenness, not violent but gentle, not quarrelsome, not a lover of money. He must manage his own family well and see that his children obey him with proper respect. (If anyone does not know how to manage his own family, how can he take care of God's church?) He must not be a recent convert, or he may become conceited and fall under the same judgment as the devil. He must also have a good reputation with outsiders, so that he will not fall into disgrace and into the devil's trap.

1 Timothy 3:1-7

DEACONS

Deacons, likewise, are to be men worthy of respect, sincere, not indulging in much wine, and not pursuing dishonest gain. They must keep hold of the deep truths of the faith with a clear conscience. They must first be tested; and then if there is nothing against them, let them serve as deacons.

In the same way, their wives are to be women worthy of respect, not malicious talkers but temperate and trustworthy in everything.

A deacon must be the husband of but one wife and must manage his children and his household well. Those who have served well gain an excellent standing and great assurance in their faith in Christ Jesus.

1 Timothy 3:8-13

CONGREGATION

CENTRAL CHURCH OF CHRIST

Amarillo, Texas

. . . a place to call home.

A SPECIAL SERVANT

Set Apart for a Special Work

1999-2000

NOMINATION FORM FOR ELDERS & DEACONS

Illustration 5a

PRESENT ELDERS

Russell Burns   Steve Rogers
Bob Crass   Shelby Stapleton
Ron Freeman   Warlick Thomas
Bill Johnson   Leon Wood
John Noyes

ELDER NOMINATION FORM

After prayerful consideration I submit the name/names of the following to serve as an elder of the Central Church of Christ.

_____

_____

_____

_____

_____

_____

signed _____

(a member of the Central Church of Christ)

A MESSAGE FROM THE ELDERS . . .

Dear Members of Our Spiritual Family,

We're calling on every family member to call on God's power and wisdom as we launch our elder and deacon selection with 55 Days of Prayer. 1999 is going to be an exciting year. In fact, we see evidence that the Lord is already causing remarkable progress and growth in our congregation.

In the early years of the church, growth created the need to select special servants called "deacons" to help carry out the church's responsibilities. According to the Bible, these men had proven to be spiritual leaders in their private lives. Because so many people are becoming involved in the Central church's ministry and because we are reaching out farther into our community and the world every day, we believe that God has provided us with many men qualified to serve as deacons in this church.

We want you to be involved in the process of identifying spiritual men in this congregation who could serve as special servants. On the next three pages you will find the Biblical qualifications for the role, the tasks for which deacons are needed, and places for you to recommend individual men.

- Prayerfully consider the qualifications of deacons as you search the congregation for men to serve.
- Suggest men for specific roles. It's fine if you can't fill in all the blanks or if you recommend the same man for several roles.
- Even though you've received only one nomination form, we encourage you to pick up one for every Christian in your family. Extra copies are available at the church building or at the foyer tables.
- Only forms with signatures will be considered.
- Return the forms to the church building on or before Wednesday night, April 28.

So you will be informed about the process involved, you should know:

Deacons will have specific assignments and be expected to:

   1) involve as many other people as possible in the area of their responsibility.

   2) report regularly to the elders.

   3) carry out their responsibilities effectively.

Deacons will serve for 12 months and then be given the opportunity to:

   1) serve another year in that role.

   2) move to another responsibility.

   3) step out of a deacon role altogether.

All men currently serving as deacons are being given these same options before the new deacons are added.

We will personally meet with the nominated men to explain their responsibilities and verify, to the best of our ability, the spiritual qualifications of each man.

Thank you for caring about the progress of this church and about the lives we can touch. Because of your concern for the service this church renders to the world and to its own, the light of Jesus Christ can shine brighter.

In his love,
The Elders

INSTRUCTIONS

1. Carefully read each job description.

2. Place the name of those you recommend on the back page.

3. The persons you recommend should meet the level of maturity set forth in I Timothy 3:1-13.

4. Recommend only those people you know personally and feel can adequately fulfill that area of special ministry. You are not expected to complete each blank.

WHAT WE EXPECT FROM DEACONS

1. A time when you let the Father talk to you daily from His word.

2. A time when you talk to Him daily through prayer about your ministry, the people in your ministry, this church, and the servant model leadership role of you and your family.

3. A demonstrated love for this church.

4. A commitment to reach the community as we meet various needs.

5. A giving of your time, talents, gifts and money as God has blessed you.

6. A time to think and dream weekly about two different ministries — the one you have now and the one you dream of having.

7. The assembly of a leadership team of people including men and women to serve as the decision makers for your ministry.

8. To assign each member of your leadership team to an individual task in your ministry.

9. To gather your ministry once a month to evaluate what is happening. Meet with an elder once a month in a Spiritual Cluster.

10. To use the staff contact assigned to your ministry as a resource person and communication tool to express your needs to the church office, ministers and elders.

11. To call the chairman of the elders or the church office by noon Tuesday if you would like to be on the Wednesday night elders' agenda.

12. To get information to the church office by noon Tuesday if you would like for this information to be in the elders' reading file on Wednesday night.

13. To contact each person who expresses an interest in working in your ministry.

14. To involve every person you can in your ministry. This includes present membership, as well as, new members God will send us.

Illustration 5b

DEACON SELECTION

Deacons, likewise, are to be men worthy of respect, sincere, not indulging in much wine, and not pursuing dishonest gain. They must keep hold of the deep truths of the faith with a clear conscience. They must first be tested; and then if there is nothing against them, let them serve as deacons.

In the same way, their wives are to be women worthy of respect, not malicious talkers but temperate and trustworthy in everything.

A deacon must be the husband of but one wife and must manage his children and his household well. Those who have served well gain an excellent standing and great assurance in their faith in Christ Jesus.

1 Timothy 3:8-13

As we select deacons, we feel convicted by God that an increasing level of spiritual maturity should be evident in those who serve in leadership roles in this church. We, as elders, state our personal commitment to a deeper level of spiritual growth here at Central.

We propose that the role of deacon be enhanced as one of greater spiritual awareness and responsibility. We are convicted by the words of I Timothy 3:8-13, and the responsibilities they imply. In our congregation these words could have the meaning:

• Men, increasingly aware of their influence in this church and community as leaders, abstaining from drinking and dishonesty in all their dealings.

• Men, joyfully and unselfishly giving their money, time and other resources.

• Men, feeling compelled to be supportive of all programs, outreach, meetings and activities of the church family.

• Men, committing to give additional time to serve in this role as special leaders.

• Men, being convicted of their roles as spiritual leaders in their families.

• Men, realizing the significance of an ever-growing and maturing relationship with Jesus Christ.

Because of our current emphasis on spiritual growth in this family, our pledge to lift up Christ and in light of scripture, we therefore urge you to "... select from among you men full of wisdom and the Holy Spirit..." (Acts 6:3-4).

Ministries of the Central Church of Christ

1. ADULT RECREATION
Provide recreational activities to draw people together and reach out to nonmembers.

2. ALCOHOL AND DRUGS
Provides prevention and training programs. Provides support groups.

3. ASSEMBLY PLANNING
This ministry works closely with the minister in planning what happens during our assemblies. Will select and work with those who are to read scriptures and give prayers at all worship services.

4. ATTENDANCE
Counts Bible Class and Worship attendance.

5. BAPTISMAL ASSISTANCE
Assist the preacher in all baptisms. Provides clothing for individuals being baptized. Arranges for ladies to assist women during baptisms at all services. Responsible for seeing the baptismal garments, towels, etc., are properly taken care of following baptisms.

6. BIBLE HOUR
Coordinates the activities relative to Children's Bible Hour.

7. BRIDGE BUILDERS
Establish a committee of approximately 20 people to plan, develop and execute programs for members 65 and over. Have special programs designed to meet the physical and spiritual needs for their members. Develops programs for regular sunshiner dinners. Encourages involvement in church affairs, including visitation of shut-ins, social affairs and Bible study.

8. BUILDING MAINTENANCE
Checks existing physical structure for maintenance such as need for painting, carpenter work, electrical work or plumbing repair. Furnishes task force to move walls in fellowship area.

---

15. To utilize training programs and retreats designed to help your ministry.

16. To help the elders with an undershepherding program.

17. To formulate a ministry program for your team. To listen to and get input from everyone in your ministry. Example: The education leadership team needs to get input from all the teachers.

18. To formulate a budget with input from everyone in your ministry.

19. To stay within your budget.

20. To get a purchase order from the office for expenditures.

21. To decorate and man a booth at a Ministry Fair each year. To explain your ministry and encourage as many people as possible to be a part of your ministry.

22. To help with the church seminars and workshops as needed.

23. To be a warm, spirit-filled person who reaches out to visitors and fellow members in this congregation with love and care.

WHAT WE PROVIDE FOR DEACONS

1. A specific ministry in which to serve to utilize your gifts for the glory of God.

2. People for you to interview to serve on your leadership team.

3. New people for you to involve in your ministry.

4. Spiritual Cluster meetings for communication and spiritual growth.

5. Staff contacts to serve as resource people for you.

6. Newsletter articles, bulletin communications and other publicity help for your ministry as you notify the church office.

7. Office help for your ministry as you coordinate a work assignment through your staff contact.

8. The counsel of elders as needed through individual counseling or a meeting with all the elders as scheduled on Wednesday night.

9. An opportunity to place communication in the elders' reading files each week.

10. Church office secretary to schedule all your events on the church calendar. She also schedules rooms as you need them for various meetings and functions.

11. Training to better equip you to serve in your ministry.

12. Men's retreats.

13. Training seminars and workshops to furnish training for you and opportunities to exchange ideas with people in similar ministries throughout the nation.

14. The opportunity for you and your ministry to plan your program and budget.

15. Freedom and trust to allow responsible people like yourself to develop your ministry.

16. Exciting, uplifting worship assemblies.

17. Quality Bible classes.

18. Groups in which to be involved.

19. Library for the use of books and tapes.

20. Visitors for you to reach out to with love on a weekly basis.

21. A philosophy dedicated to meeting the needs of people in this community and church through ministry.

22. People to help you with your ministry upon your request.

23. A brochure listing all the leaders in your ministry to be given to every member of this congregation to enhance the communication process.

Illustration 5c

9. CARE MINISTRY
This is a ministry of caring, love and concern. They strive to reach first time attenders and visitors. Also, coordinate Sunday night Care Groups.

10. CHILDREN'S SINGING AND DRAMA
Develops children's singing, puppet, and drama groups.

11. CHRISTIAN CAMPS AND RETREATS
Encourages our youth and adults to participate in this. Helps coordinate activities in this area.

12. CHURCH GROWTH
What makes a church grow? This ministry was created for the purpose of researching all facets of church growth. It will eventually serve as a resource for many of the other ministries.

13. CHURCH OFFICE VOLUNTEERS
Recruits and encourages many church office volunteers.

14. COMMUNICATIONS
This ministry's function is to communicate through every means possible — newspaper, brochures, billboards, posters, radio, television — what Christianity is all about at Central.

15. COMMUNITY CARE
Provides food and clothing for needy. Involves church in events such as "Sack Sunday." Works with High Plains Food Bank. Works to provide Blood Bank reserve.

16. COMMUNITY OUTREACH
This ministry seeks to create an atmosphere at Central which leads to the involvement of each member in leading people to Christ. They are responsible for home Bible studies.

17. COUNSELING
Provides support for our counseling program, working closely with our counselor. Provides Family Enrichment classes, seminars, and retreats.

18. CONTRIBUTION
See that contributions and special funds are collected at all services.

19. DISCIPLING
Provides intense training for those who want to be close followers of Jesus.

20. DIVORCE CARE
Helps people spiritually heal who have been through a divorce.

21. EDUCATION — ADULT
Works with education director to coordinate and develop the adult education program.

22. EDUCATION — CHILDREN
Works with education directors and supervisors to develop the children's education program.

23. EDUCATION — YOUTH
Works with youth minister and supervisors to develop the youth education program.

24. FAMILY
Provides training and opportunities to help us have strong Christian families.

25. FAMILY CARE
This ministry is responsible for financial support of all those under the oversight of our elders, ensuring that we have "no needy" among us. This ministry advises and assists family members in times of emergency. It also recruits "Good Samaritans" and helps with employment.

26. FAMILY LIFE GROUPS
Responsible for our once a month small group Bible studies in homes. Integrates new people into groups and works with our shepherding program.

27. FELLOWSHIP DINNERS
Congregational Fellowships — Plan and coordinate all activities: Year End — Date, time, menu, food, serving, place, decorations, clean up, ticket sales, entertainment and any other details.

28. FINANCE
This ministry coordinates our annual budget preparation. It also monitors our financial progress throughout the year and insures financial responsibility.

29. GREETERS
Arrives at the assigned services 15 minutes prior to the beginning of the worship hour. Arranges for a minimum of three people to greet at each worship service. Secures substitutes for absentees. Greets each individual by name, if possible, at the assigned entrance. Greeter must be alert for new members and visitors. Distributes "order of worship" sheets at morning services.

30. GRIEF RECOVERY
Contacts those who have lost loved ones, and provides grief recovery seminars.

31. GROUND MAINTENANCE
Cares for plants in and around the building, as well as, along streets, alleys and property lines of parking lots. Is responsible for weed control and maintenance of parking stripes on the lots. Responsible to see that sidewalks and entrances are free of ice and snow during winter storms.

32. HALL MONITORS
Assigns workers to monitor the halls during worship and Bible classes. Assists in directing members and visitors to classes.

33. HIGH PLAINS CHILDREN'S HOME
Works with children's home group attending Central to provide support for houseparents and maximum spiritual growth for youth.

34. HOSPITAL VISITATION
Provides a team to visit people in our local hospitals. Report family needs to proper source.

35. INVOLVEMENT
This ministry strives to identify the interests and talents and gifts of our members and match them with an appropriate ministry. They are dedicated to the principle of helping everyone find their place in the body. This responsibility includes the assimilation of new members.

36. JAIL & PRISON MINISTRY
Shares the Gospel with those in jail and prison. Provides emotional and counseling support for families. Works with prison ministry. Provides Bible lessons for inmates.

37. LEADERSHIP TRAINING FOR CHRIST
Provides leadership training for our children.

38. LIBRARY
The Library Ministry is responsible for the purchase of new books and categorizing of these and other incoming books.

39. LIGHTING AND SOUND
Operates lighting and sound for assemblies and special events.

40. LORD'S TABLE SERVICE
Selects men to serve the Lord's Supper. Obtains substitutes for those not present. Keeps records pertaining to those willing to serve and those who have served. Appoints individuals in charge for each service to line up volunteers and select substitutes. Oversee the preparation and clean up for communion.

41. LORD'S SUPPER FOR SHUTINS
Take communion to those who are unable to attend services.

42. MEDIA
Provide media equipment and personnel for media presentations. Provide personnel and media presentations for auditorium services.

43. MENS MINISTRY
Encourage men to be spiritual leaders in their homes.

44. MISSIONS
Coordinates our World Bible School and Mission activities. Keeps congregation informed about our mission program.

45. NEW MEMBER ASSIMILATION
Keeps rosters of new members to ensure their assimilation into the Central body. Uses a key couple or single individual to assist the new member by providing friendship, companionship and an understanding of any problems. Finds out if new members are potential Bible class teachers or are experienced in any other phase of the work. Provide a special welcome to all new members by hosting new members in their homes for meals.

Illustration 5d

The Key Is the
Ministry System

Each one should use whatever gift he has received to serve others, faithfully administering God's grace in its various forms.
1 Peter 4:10

C O N G R E G A T I O N

M I N I S T E R S

E L D E R S

DEACON-LED MINISTRIES
A. Minister Leader
B. Leadership Team
Composed of 10-20 men and women
C. Many of the people involved in ministry but not as decision makers.

WOMEN'S MINISTRIES
A. Ministry Team
B. Leadership Team
C. Others

SINGLES
A. Ministry Leaders
B. Leadership Team
C. Others

TASK FORCES
A. Task Force Leader
B. Project Team
C. Others

A BIBLICAL PLAN TO
INVOLVE EVERY MEMBER

We're in the people business at the Central Church of Christ. We strive in every way possible to let Christ work through us so our Lord can be magnified. We've developed a unique Biblical structure called the Ministry System which features a plan to involve every member. Ministries are led by ministry leaders and a leadership team of men and women who are the decision makers. They strive to involve everyone in the congregation who is interested in their particular ministry. Everyone is someone special in the Central family.

EPHESIANS 4

WHO: God chose you to be His people (v. 1).

WHAT: Christ gave each one of us a special gift (v. 7).

WHY: Christ gave those gifts to prepare God's Holy people for the work of serving (v. 12).

WHEN: Each part does its own work (v. 16).

RESULTS: This makes the whole body grow and be strong with love (v. 16).

MESSAGE: Say what people need . . . words that will help others become stronger (v. 29).

SPECIAL NOTE TO
ALL MEMBERS

The elders will be adding new ministries to take care of the needs of our fast-growing family.

1. Please list below areas of additional work needed in this church family.

_____

_____

2. List the major areas in which you are currently involved:

_____

_____

3. List any new area in which you would like to be included:

_____

_____

Your name: _____

Address: _____

City/Zip: _____

Phone: _____

The majority of our ministries are led by deacons who are nominated by the congregation to serve for one year in their specific area of expertise and interest. Leadership teams of 10 to 20 people are composed of both men and women.

There are also women's ministries which only include women and singles ministries which only include singles. Task forces are appointed to fulfill special short-term projects. These are normally completed in less than a year, but occasionally grow into a long-term ministry.

---

55. TAPE MINISTRY
Tapes services, duplicates and sends out weekly to shut-ins and people who request tapes. Keeps supply of tapes on hand for use. Orders special tapes to be kept in media room.

56. TRANSPORTATION
Provides rides to church services and activities.

57. UNDERSHEPHERDS
Help our elders with shepherding. Work in the prevention of dropouts.

58. USHERS
Help people find seats during our services. Also provide a way to recognize and greet visitors. May be called upon to usher at special events.

59. VISITATION SPECIAL
Monitors and coordinates activities involved in an active visitation program for Central shut-ins. Coordinates this activity with the Bridge Builders group. Works in the hospital visitation program.

60. WELCOME HOME
Utilizes supper clubs to invite new members into homes.

61. WELCOME PARDNER
Gets printed material to every person who moves to Amarillo. Provides follow up from the list.

62. YOUNG ADULTS
This ministry coordinates all phases of our program for young adults.

63. YOUTH
Works with youth minister to develop Huddle groups and the youth program.

---

46. NURSERY AND CHILD CARE
Develops and maintains a quality childcare program.

47. PARKING AND TRAFFIC
Directs those who are seeking a parking place. Encourages those trying to park in the immediate church lot not to use those facilities which are reserved for handicapped and elderly people. Assign young people to help by opening doors, carrying babies, etc.

48. PERSONAL FINANCE
Provides free counseling to members needing financial advice.

49. PRAISE TEAMS
Provides and trains singing groups for our second service.

50. PRAYER
Encourages Central family to spend more time in prayer. Coordinate prayer room.

51. SINGLES AND COLLEGE PROGRAMS
This ministry will coordinate all phases of the singles and college programs such as: organizational structure, spiritual growth, class activities, Bible study, fellowship activities, visitation program, retreats and development of leadership. Provides Divorce Recovery Seminars.

52. SPECIAL EVENTS
Works with staff coordinator in the coordination of special events for the Central Church family.

53. SPECIAL MUSIC
Furnishes singers for weddings and funerals. Develops special groups and provides special training.

54. SUPPORT GROUPS
Works with the Support Groups which are organized through the adult Bible classes — to help each member of the Central family to belong and find support for their faith and Christian life.

Illustration 5e

Illustration 6

Affirmation of Elders
Individual Response Form

It is my desire that the following men serve as elders and shepherds of the
[NAME OF CONGREGATION]

(Name 1)	(Name 2)	(Name 3)
Yes ☐ No ☐	Yes ☐ No ☐	Yes ☐ No ☐

(Name 4)	(Name 5)	(Name 6)
Yes ☐ No ☐	Yes ☐ No ☐	Yes ☐ No ☐

I have expressed my personal desire above, knowing this will contribute to determining who will lead this congregation as elders.

I believe the Scriptures teach that God is at work in this process because Acts 20:28 states that those men chosen by the congregation for leadership are made overseers of the flock of God by the Holy Spirit.

Therefore, I submit myself to the will of the congregation as a whole, and I will support, respect, and honor all those shepherds chosen this day.

Please check the following about yourself:

☐ Male
☐ Female

☐ Married
☐ Single

Age Bracket
☐ Youth
☐ 20-30
☐ 31-40
☐ 41-50
☐ 51-60
☐ 61 +

Years at (this congregation)
☐ 0-2
☐ 2-4
☐ 4-6
☐ 6-8
☐ 8-10
☐ 10 +

During our recent time of nominating men to serve as elders the following men were listed numerous times. Our present elders have interviewed them and would like to recommend that these men serve as elders. If you have any Biblical objection to these men serving as elders, please go to [ ] personally or contact [ ] of our present elders [ ] here are no valid objections, these [ ] will be installed as el[ ]on (Date).

[Name 1]   [Name 2]   [Name 3]

INSTRUCTIONS

All current deacons will continue to serve unless they wish to resign. A list of their names is included in this brochure.

Please list the names of additional men you would like to have serve as deacons on this page.

Person Nominated	Suggested Ministry
1.	
2.	
3.	
4.	
5.	
6.	
7.	
8.	
9.	
10.	
11.	
12.	
13.	
14.	
15.	
16.	
17.	
18.	
19.	
20.	

PRESENT DEACONS

Gary Antonelli	Jeff Eggleston	George Owen
Marvin Arbeiter	Wayne Fair	Jeff Perkins
Kelly Archer	Alex Fairly	John Richardson
Mike Barber	Mike Fisher	Mike Robertson
Alford Blount	John Francies	Warren Sanders
Eddie Brasher	Craig Gladman	Dale Scott
Travis Brown	Tom Glass	Mark Speck
Tom Burdett	Thomas Graham	Cary Speer
John Burgtorf	Dickie Haney	Frank Stepp
Steve Butler	Jake Holster	George Stewart
Jim Carver	Carl Holtman	George Terry
Terry Carver	Ronnie Hudson	Bruce Tidmore
Don Case	Brice Kelley	Andrew Tonne
Eric Cato	Lee Kendle	Pat Treat
Steve Cearley	Michael Kennedy	Kelly Ulsinger
Mike Cherry	Cary Ladd	James Vaughan
John Todd Cornett	Robin Liles	Johnny Vaughan
Mark Cosgrove	Mark Love	Dale Wesley
Iman Crawford	Greg Lusk	Warren West
Larry Cunyus	Don Moore	Mike Williams
Wayland Danile	Dean Morgan	Randy Wilson
Lee Donaway	Lanny Newton	Steve Wood
Gary Douglass	Steve Nordyke	Bob Wright
		Keith Wynn

given a notebook. The notebook included each church leader's name and ministry and a list of our values, mission and vision (see illustration 2f in the Welcome Class package in chapter 5). Since we have two different types of Sunday morning services, we stressed the importance of unity. We said we could have unity with a dozen different services if they all enhanced our values, mission, and vision. An outline of the orientation follows (illustration 7a), along with some of the material in the notebook. The Mates Spiritual Awareness game (illustration 7c) is played like "The Newlywed Game." Each mate is supposed to put down what their mate would put down.

God's Team Prays and Serves

"For I know the plans I have for you," declares the LORD, "plans to prosper you and not to harm you, plans to give you hope and a future" (Jeremiah 29:11).

1. Dick's Devotional — "The Parable of the Goose"
2. Season of Prayer — Frank
3. The Vision, Mission and Values of Central — Bob
4. God Calls Teams Together — Ray
5. Future Equipping Opportunities — Kyle
6. Prayer with mate.

Illustration 7a

MATES SPIRITUAL AWARENESS GAME

1. Favorite book in Old Testament. _____

2. Favorite book in New Testament. _____

3. Excluding Jesus, favorite man in the Bible. _____

4. Favorite woman in the Bible. _____

5. Favorite verse in the Bible. _____

6. Favorite religious song. _____

7. Favorite time to study the Bible. _____

8. Favorite time to pray. _____

9. Person at Central most likely to go to with a big problem. _____
_____

10. Number of souls you think will be attending Central in A.D. 2010. _____

5 Goose Sense Facts

Fact 1: As each goose flaps its wings, it creates an "uplift" for the birds that follow. By flying in "V" formation, the whole flock adds 71 percent greater flying range than if each bird flew alone. *Lesson:* People who share a common direction and sense of community can get where they are going more quickly and easily because they are traveling on the thrust of one another.

Fact 2: When a goose falls out of formation, it suddenly feels the drag and resistance of flying alone. It quickly moves back into formation to take advantage of the lifting power of the bird immediately in front of it. *Lesson:* If we have as much sense as a goose, we will stay in formation with those headed where we want to go. We are willing to accept their help and give help to others.

Fact 3: When the lead goose tires, it rotates back into the formation and another goose flies into the point position. *Lesson:* It pays to take turns doing the hard tasks and sharing leadership. As with geese, people are interdependent on each other's skills, capabilities, and unique arrangements of gifts, talents, or resources.

Fact 4: The geese flying in formation honk to encourage those in front to keep up their speed. *Lesson:* We need to make sure our honking is encouraging. In groups where there is encouragement, the production is greater.

Fact 5: When a goose gets sick, wounded, or shot down, two geese drop out of formation and follow it down to help or protect it. They stay with it until it dies or is able to fly again. Then they launch out with another formation or catch up with the flock. *Lesson:* If we have as much sense as a goose, we will stand by each other in difficult times as well as when we are strong.

MINISTRY EXPENDITURE REQUEST FORM

MINISTRY:

ITEM REQUEST	PAYABLE TO	BUDGET ACCOUNT NUMBER	AMOUNT
		TOTAL	

DATE REQUESTED: DATE NEEDED:

COMMENTS:

CHECK REQUESTED BY:

_____   _____
APPROVAL (FINANCE COMMITTEE)   *DATE*

Let's Dream and Plan!
Strategy for Local Congregations

1. Write a sentence of less than ten words which describes your ministry.

2. What one word best describes your ministry?

3. What are two or three Bible verses which you would give as reasons for your ministry.

4. What kind of leadership team people are you trying to assemble?

5. What would be some of their specific assignments?

6. What are some good ways to involve new people in your ministry?

7. How do elders, deacons, and ministers best communicate?

8. How do you best communicate with the congregation?

9. What are your ministry's major goals for this year?

10. What is the best way to prepare and present the budget?

Prayer Leads Us to Use Our Gifts

Prayer is the driving force which leads us to use our gifts for the glory of God. In the nominations for elders and deacons, we had 55 days of prayer before these men were chosen. Elders individually meet with prospective deacons and their wives in the deacon's home to pray with them. Half the orientation period is spent in prayer. Every new member is given a prayer partner by the prayer ministry. Our first goal is for new members to be praying members who know Jesus.

> Every new member is given a prayer partner by the prayer ministry.

Now we are ready to teach them to serve. Jesus said "The greatest among you will be your servant" (Matt. 23:11). A great illustration of this is how we teach this principle to our youth. At the beginning of the school year, we have all of our youth and adults in the auditorium for a special Bible class. We have the new sixth graders in the youth program now. We are trying to teach them to serve, and we are trying to break down barriers between the youth. This last year 48 of our seniors went up to the stage in front of 1,000 adults and other youth. They then called 48 sixth graders to the stage to introduce them to the youth program. The 48 seniors went behind stage and got 48 towels and wash pans. Then, these 48 seniors individually washed the sixth graders' feet and dried them! It was so quiet you could hear a pin drop! What a lesson! Barriers between different ages had been broken down and these new sixth graders were learning to serve as servants. Then, with all the youth on their knees, the seniors and sixth graders joined hands and prayed together.

Think it over: Are there other practical ways you can devise for teaching servanthood? Would this idea work for you?

121

The prayer ministry, elders, and involvement ministry should pray by name for each new member. They should pray that each new member will use his gifts for the glory of God. *The Servant-Driven Church* has details about how to involve every member.

Do this:

Determine what areas of involvement are available in your congregation, then plan ways to communicate these service opportunities.

With the coming of the new millennium, we need to use every available means in every available way to involve every available soul. This means that a church needs to have a web site to show ways people can get involved in a ministry. E-mail should be used in the involvement process. Fax machines and telephone calls to each new member will be useful. Fifteen minute cassette and video tapes can present the story of the ministries for the local church and ways people can be involved.

> We need to use every available means in every available way to involve every available soul.

These can be delivered to each home. Involvement or welcome classes can be conducted Sunday morning, Sunday night and Wednesday night. In a previous chapter, we talked about our Sunday morning goal of caring, Sunday night goal of connecting, and Wednesday night goal of equipping. We should try to get new members in a Sunday morning class that really cares about them, a Sunday night group where they connect, and a Wednesday class where they are equipped. The prayer ministry should connect with them in prayer.

The Sunday morning Bible class and Sunday night small groups can do a tremendous job of involving people. The class and small group can function like a mini-congregation to involve people. An example would be as follows:

1. Greeters
2. Pass out prayer request cards
3. Get prayer leaders
4. Form prayer partners
5. Fellowship activities
6. Special projects such as missions or food for needy

7. Group leader
8. Attendance and follow up
9. Contact new members
10. Teach
11. Make refreshments and clean up crew
12. Visit sick and bereaved
13. Food for sick and bereaved
14. Communications person (letters, e-mail, phone call chain, etc.)

Sermons, classes, and small groups can also teach a series of lessons on involvement. Forms can be passed out as a recruiting tool to involve people. Youth can be trained and paired with adult ministry leaders for equipping.

After the names of all involvement prospects are entered into the church computer, the material needs to be passed on to the ministry leaders. These ministry leaders should contact these prospects as soon as possible to get them involved in their ministry.

Accountability for this is accomplished by Spiritual Cluster Meetings. Elders divide the ministries up and have their groups in their homes once a month. Both husbands and wives attend. Elders are mentors and models of the "fruit of the spirit" at these meetings. They primarily listen, encourage, and offer advice when it is solicited. Each ministry member will share what's happening in his ministry. Elders will also ask if they are getting new people involved in their ministries because this is a primary goal. We don't want the ministry leaders just doing the work themselves. This is described in detail in *The Servant-Driven Church*. Elders give a short, written report of these meetings to the involvement minister or some involvement leaders. This helps him keep up with accomplishments, needs, and problems in each ministry. The involvement ministry needs to make phone calls at one-month, 3-month, 6-month, 9-month and one-year

Prayer is living with the unexplainable.

intervals to find out the following things from new members:

For you to consider: What kind of follow-up for visitors and new members is in place in your church? What could you do you are not doing?

1. Have you attended the welcome class or an involvement class?
2. Are you attending a Sunday morning Bible class?
3. Which service are you attending?
4. Are you involved in a ministry?
5. Do you have a prayer partner?
6. Have you eaten in the preacher's home? (The size of the church may require dividing the group to several homes such as elders or associate ministers.)
7. Do you know a shepherd?
8. Are you meeting in a small group?
9. Have you taken an evaluation of your spiritual gifts?
10. How are you and your family doing spiritually?
11. Do you have any special needs?

Many people are looking for ways to discover their gifts and use them to the glory of God. This is especially true of those under the age of 40. Once again the val-

> Many people, especially those under the age of 40, are looking for ways to discover their gifts and use them to the glory of God.

ues, mission, and vision of the church need to be emphasized at this time so these new people can get excited about using their gifts as they help fulfill these overall goals.

Here are some useful gifts evaluations and involvement programs to look at: (Examples of many of these are in *The Servant-Driven Church*).

1. 10-minute gifts survey from Guidance Assistance Programs, Box 105, Winfield, IL 60190.
2. 10-minute evaluation of what really motivates people (same address as above).
3. Networking Program by Willow Creek in Chicago. Willow Creek Association, P.O. Box 3188, Barrington, IL 60011-3188.

4. Mission Viejo's 4-bases program with Rick Warren's *The Purpose Driven Church*. Published by Zondervan.
5. Richland Hills Spiritual Gifts Survey, 6300 N.E. Loop 820, Ft. Worth, TX, 76180.
6. Larry Gilbert's Team Ministry Material. Church Growth Institute, P.O. Box 4404, Lynchburg, VA 24502.
7. Dr. John Maxwell's Injoy Material on Lay Ministry, P.O. Box 7700, Atlanta, GA, 30357-0700.
8. Uniquely You Material by Dr. Mels Carbonell. Uniquely You, P.O. Box 490, Blue Ridge, GA 30513.

By far, the most detailed spiritual gifts material I have seen is the Uniquely You material developed by Dr. Mels Carbonell. Mels was reared in Cuba and his Dad was a Communist leader who helped stop the Bay of Pigs invasion. His unusual name, Mels is unique as he was named after four Communist leaders.

Marx

Engels

Lenin

Stalin

While in high school, he and his friend stole a Bible out of a motel. The Bible had been placed there by the Gideons. Someone had offered to give anyone a thousand dollar bill if they could prove the Bible scientifically inaccurate. Mels would read the Bible every night and go to his science teacher each day at school with a point from the Bible that might be wrong. The science teacher kept telling him every day that the Bible was scientifically correct in each area he asked about. He studied himself out of Communism and became a follower of God. To the disgust of his parents, he told them he was going to attend Bob Jones University and become a minister! This is what he did!

He has developed four different gifts profiles which can be computer graded, analyzed and evaluated.

The profiles are for 7 gifts, 9 gifts, 16 gifts and 23 gifts. Detailed descriptions are given of each gift. He gives the major goal of each gift and danger of the gift when it is overused.

Examine yourself: Where does your own personality fit in this type of analysis? How about other members of your family?

He then combines the gifts with the DISC Model of Human Behavior. Understanding this four-temperament model helps us understand why people do what they do. "D" behavior is dominant, direct, demanding and decisive. This personality, traditionally known as the "choleric" temperament, is active and task oriented like Paul. The "I" behavior is inspiring, influencing, impressing and inducing. This "sanguine" personality is very active and people-oriented like Peter. The "S" behavior is submissive, steady, stable, and security oriented. This "phlegmatic" personality is passive and people oriented like Moses. The "C" behavior is competent, compliant, cautious, and calculating. This "melancholic" personality is passive and task oriented like Thomas. Naturally, there are many blends of these traits. The chart and interpretation developed by Dr. Carbonell are reproduced on the facing page.

Dr. Carbonell does an outstanding job explaining where your spiritual gifts can be used most effectively. One of his charts has been included (p. 84) in the February 14 lesson plan.

He then combines an Involvement/Personality Perspective (page after next) to explain how involvement and personality profile work together.

Dr. Carbonell is extraordinarily accurate in explaining in which ministry people should serve when their spiritual gifts profiles are combined with their personality profiles.

He has additional material on Leadership Insights and how people act under pressure. He has super material on how to handle and resolve conflicts. Some of his other excellent material covers Change Management, Predicting Responses and Avoiding Conflicts, and Team Building.

Interpretation . . .

Be sure to first complete the ❶ *Uniquely You Questionnaire.* Follow the instructions at the top of page. Remember to choose a focus (home or work) as you respond.

You have a predictable pattern of behavior because you have a specific personality. There are four basic personality types. These types, also known as temperaments, blend together to determine your unique personality. To help you understand why you often feel, think and act the way you do, the following graphic summarizes the Four Temperament Model of Human Behavior.

Active / Task-oriented

"D" — Dominating, directing, driving, demanding, determined, decisive, doing.

Active / Outgoing

Active / People-oriented

"I" — Inspiring, influencing, inducing, impressing, interactive, interested in people.

Task

D | I

C | S

People

Passive / Task-oriented

"C" — Cautious, competent, calculating, compliant, careful, contemplative.

Passive / Reserved

Passive / People-oriented

"S" — Steady, stable, shy, security-oriented, servant, submissive, specialist.

"D" BEHAVIOR / Biblical Example: Paul
(Active / Task-oriented) Known as "Choleric"
Descriptions: *Dominant, Direct, Demanding, Decisive,*
Basic Motivation: Challenge and Control
Desires: • Freedom from control • Authority • Varied Activities • Difficult Assignments • Opportunities for Advancement • Choices, rather than ultimatums
Responds Best To Leader Who: • Provides direct answers • Sticks to task • Gets to the point • Provides pressure • Allows freedom for personal accomplishments
Needs To Learn: • You need people • Relaxation is not a crime • Some controls are needed • Everyone has a boss • Self-control is most important • To focus on finishing well is important • Sensitivity to people's feelings is wise.
Biblical Advice: BE GENTLE / NOT BOSSY—*Wisdom from above is . . . gentle,* James 3:17 • CONTROL YOUR FEELINGS AND ACTIONS—*Be angry and sin not,* Eph. 4:26 • FOCUS ON ONE THING AT A TIME—*This ONE thing I do,* Phil. 3:13 • HAVE A SERVANT'S ATTITUDE—*By love, serve one another,* Gal. 5:13.

"I" BEHAVIOR / Biblical Example: Peter
(Active / People-oriented) Known as "Sanguine"
Descriptions: *Inspiring, Influencing, Impressing, Inducing,*
Basic Motivation: Recognition and Approval
Desires: • Prestige • Friendly relationships • Freedom from details • Opportunities to help others • Opportunities to motivate others • Chance to verbalize ideas
Responds Best To Leader Who: • Is fair and also a friend • Provides social involvement • Provides recognition of abilities • Offers rewards for risk-taking
Needs To Learn: • Time must be managed- Deadlines are important • Too much optimism can be dangerous • Being responsible is more important than being popular • Listening better will improve one's influence.
Biblical Advice: BE HUMBLE / AVOID PRIDE—*Humble yourself in the SIGHT of God,* James 3:17 • CONTROL YOUR SPEECH—*Be quick to hear, slow to speak,* James 1:19 • BE MORE ORGANIZED—*Do all things decently and in order,* 1 Cor. 14:40 • BE PATIENT —*The fruit of the Spirit is . . . longsuffering,* Gal. 5:23.

"C" BEHAVIOR / Biblical Example: Thomas
(Passive / Task-oriented) Known as "Melancholy"
Descriptions: *Competent, Compliant, Cautious, Calculating*
Basic Motivation: Quality and Correctness
Desires: • Clearly defined tasks • Details • Limited risks • Assignments that require precision and planning • Time to think
Responds Best To Leader Who: • Provides reassurance • Spells out detailed operating procedures • Provides resources to do task correctly • Listens to suggestions
Needs To Learn: • Total support is not always possible • Thorough explanation is not everything • Deadlines must be met • More optimism will lead to greater success.
Biblical Advice: BE MORE POSITIVE—*Whatsoever things are lovely, of good report ... think on these things,* Phil. 4:8 • AVOID A BITTER AND CRITICAL SPIRIT—*Let all bitterness . . . be put away from you,* Eph. 4:11 • BE JOYFUL —*The fruit of the Spirit is . . . joy,* Gal. 5:22 • DON'T WORRY—*Fret not,* Psa. 37:1.

"S" BEHAVIOR / Biblical Example: Moses
(Passive / People-oriented) Known as "Phlegmatic"
Descriptions: *Submissive, Steady, Stable, Security-oriented*
Basic Motivation: Stability and Support
Desires: • An area of specialization • Identification with a group • Established work patterns • Security of situation • Consistent familiar environment
Responds Best To Leader Who: • Is relaxed and friendly • Allows time to adjust to changes • Allows to work at own pace • Gives personal support
Needs To Learn: • Change provides opportunity • Friendship isn't everything • Discipline is good • Boldness and Taking risks is sometimes necessary
Biblical Advice: BE BOLD AND STRONG—*Only be strong and very courageous,* Joshua 1:6 • BE CONFIDENT AND FEAR-LESS—*God has not given you the spirit of fear,* 2 Tim. 1:7 • BE MORE ENTHUSIASTIC—*Whatsoever you do, do it HEARTILY as unto the Lord,* Col. 3:23.

Involvement / Personality Perspective

Where your personality can be used most effectively!

My highest plotting point:
Graph 1 ___ ; Graph 2 ___ ;

My next hightest plotting
points are:
Graph 1 ___ ; Graph 2 ___ .

1. First give God your "giftedness" to use for His glory.
2. Read the sections of D, I, S or C and Spiritual Gifts influences on the *Interpretation* page which correspond with your highest plotting points on your Graphs 1 & 2.
3. Look for opportunities for ministry to use your "giftedness" —
   • Search the Scriptures for insights on how God can use you.
   • Ask your minister or mature Christian friend to guide you.
4. Get involved in a ministry ASAP.
5. Pray God will control you and make you *"all things to all men."*

"D" BEHAVIOR *(Active / Task-oriented)*

Abilities: Lead, take stand, confront issue, persevere, dictate, make decisions and control.

Opportunities: Organize needed ministry, chair Stewardship Committee, head Usher's Committee, commit to specific challenge.

Warning: You want to control everyone, but must first control yourself. Remember, *"to have authority, you must be under authority."* Be loyal to your leaders.

Reward: Follow your spiritual leaders. Allow Christ to be the Lord of your life, and God will use you in a great way to move the ministry forward.

Prayer: *"Dear God, control my driving, demanding and dominant personality, so I can be a strong and peace-making leader for your glory."*

"I" BEHAVIOR *(Active / People-oriented)*

Abilities: Communicate, inspire, influence, make friends, optimism, enthusiasm.

Opportunities: Give public testimony, drama, social committee, greeter, encourager, lead discussion group and visitation.

Warning: You naturally outshine others. Don't serve purely through your *"personality."* Also, pride and sinful lusts will destroy your testimony.

Reward: God designed you to shine for Him. When you allow Him to shine through you, He will use you in greater ways than you ever imagined.

Prayer: *"Dear God, keep me humble to do your will, not mine. Help me give you and those who praise me the credit for all You have done."*

"C" BEHAVIOR *(Passive / Task-oriented)*

Abilities: Analyze, improve, discern, calculate, follow directions, do the right thing.

Opportunities: Finance Committee, long-range planning, office, record information, research, teach, organize and order curriculum.

Warning: Due to your cautiousness, criticism comes easy. Don't always be pessimistic and hard to convince. Increase your faith in God and trust those you follow.

Reward: Ministers need competent people to fulfill their visions. You can be a great blessing if you continually look at the possibilities, rather than impossibilities.

Prayer: *"Dear God, help me be optimistic in the midst of problems — a source of encouragement to those who find faith and victory difficult."*

"S" BEHAVIOR *(Passive / People-oriented)*

Abilities: Support, serve, specialize, finish what others start, work behind the scenes, do what needs to be done.

Opportunities: On call whenever needed, hospital visitation, encourage new members, office, keep records, telephoning and counseling.

Warning: Shyness hinders your opportunities to do great things for God. Be more aggressive and assertive. Be careful, people may take advantage of you.

Reward: Believing God's promise that you can do all things through Him who strengthens you, step out and try the difficult. You may be surprised what God can do.

Prayer: *"Dear God, I know you use the weak things to confound the mighty and I often don't feel capable of serving you, but through your grace I will."*

Everyone: You should never use your personality as an excuse not to do what God commands everyone to do. For example, the Bible commands you to do the work of an evangelist. "D"s and "I"s may feel more comfortable talking to people about Christ, while "S"s and "C"s may not. Yet everyone should share the *good news.* "S"s may feel more comfortable working behind the scenes, but God may call a "S", like Moses, to lead a group. Or God may call an "I" to work behind the scenes. You must learn to *"be all things to all men that we might by all means save some."* **Whatever you do, do it through Christ. Read Gal. 2:20.**

All of this material is incredible if you want to develop a spiritual gifts ministry. I hope I have whetted your appetite to call Dr. Carbonell with Uniquely You, attend his seminars for training and certification and utilize these great tools in your local church. His phone number is 706-492-5490 and fax number is 706-492-3484.

These charts are used here by permission.

Consider: What practical uses can you think of for this kind of analysis in putting people to work for the church?

8 Prayer Drives Us to Meet the Needs of Others

This chapter is for the church leader who spends many hours on his knees in prayer trying to meet the needs of the people in the congregation and in the community. He knows he is to "feed the flock" and "tend the flock," but he cannot do this until he understands their needs. This chapter will provide valuable help for discovering these needs.

Let's first look at spiritual gifts. Spiritual gifts are gifts from God to individual members. We need to feed and develop all of these gifts so we can have a balanced church to serve the needs of the church and the community.

> The prayerful leader knows he is to "feed the flock" and "tend the flock," but he cannot do this until he understands their needs.

The nine basic gifts which are given to believers by the Holy Spirit are

1. Evangelist—These people share the gospel with others and get results. They are very comfortable in doing this.
2. Prophet—These members have the ability to discern right from wrong. They point out wrongs in both the church and the community. They can be opinionated and traditional.
3. Teacher—These people are in-depth teachers of the word.
4. Exhorter—These folks are encouragers. They are not very interested in an in-depth study, but they want all parts of the service to work together in

harmony. They like to encourage people to work and serve together in practical ways.

5. Pastor-Teachers love to shepherd the flock. They are interested in people and relationships with people. They love to provide relational leadership.

6. Mercy Show-ers give empathy and sympathy to the hurting. They reflect on what it would be like to have the problems of these people, and they identify with them.

7. Servers like to help anyone. They will help them any way they can for any good cause. They like to work behind the scenes.

8. Givers like to use their stewardship to further God's kingdom. They like to make a difference in today's world by taking on significant projects. They don't understand why other people don't give more.

9. Administrators like to put everything together so the church can function efficiently and effectively. They are good at seeing the big picture, organizing, and delegating tasks.

If a local church is a balanced church, all of these God-given gifts will be fed and developed. Many churches are unbalanced. If a church is primarily evangelistic, they convert people — but they go right out the back door. A church may have quality, in-depth Bible school teachers, but they may not connect with the needs of many of the people. A church may be filled with prophets who spend most of their time pointing out what's wrong with the church and the world.

The following chart shows the greatest interests of people with these gifts. It's easy to see where they work together and where they have more difficulty working together. Shepherds of a balanced church try to use the assemblies, Bible classes, small groups and ministries to feed and develop people with all their gifts. The chart looks like this (next page):

Do this: Try to relate your own primary interests to one of the lists of spiritual gifts. Are you fulfilling your gift?

Needs as Viewed by the Various "Gifts"

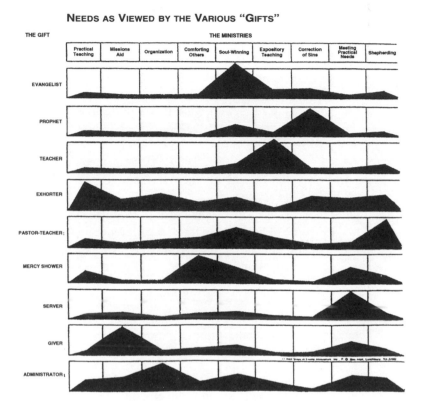

Church leaders also need to study systems-sensitive leadership. Mike Armour has written an in-depth book on this topic and encourages us to feed and empower diversity in these systems without polarizing the church. He takes the eight thinking systems uncovered in the research of Clare Graves and applies this to the church. These systems are important because they give us a distinctive outlook on life. They do the following things:

1. Define our sense of who we are.
2. Organize our lives.
3. Group our priorities.
4. Structure relationships
5. Help us analyze ideas.

6. Determine how we respond to innovation and change.

Dr. Graves also discovered these general principles about the eight thinking systems.

1. At birth, all eight systems are latent within us.
2. They activate, one by one, at various stages of existence.
2. No one relies equally on all eight systems. Nor do we use them all simultaneously.
3. Of the eight systems, one or two will always be so influential that they dominate our personal outlook.
4. Any system or combination of systems can be dominant. The choice is not prescripted.
5. For that reason, dominant systems vary from person to person.
6. They also change as we move through various phases of personal development.

Dominant systems are highly dynamic. They present themselves in ever-changing patterns, both in the lives of individuals and among the members of a group. Mike Armour states that the ability to recognize that dynamic and understand it is the cornerstone of systems-sensitive leadership.

These eight thinking systems are world-wide as well as be-ing located in our local communities and churches. These eight different groups include:

1. *Survival* — This group has been devastated and they are just living one day at a time. They may be divorced, out of a job, spiritually dry, or have marital, physical or emotional problems.

2. *Safety* — This group wants to be part of something that lets them feel safe. They want to be part of something that is

> Prayer is refusing to worry when I don't have a clue as to what God would have me do with my life.

Consider carefully: As you read through the descriptions of the systems, ask yourself where you fit, keeping in mind the general principles above.

routine and predictable. Their motto is "Don't change things!"

3. *Strength and Power* — This group looks for security in strength and they will follow strong leadership. They are primarily interested in themselves and they are not great team players. They want services, classes and programs which primarily meet their needs.

4. *Truth* — This group likes everything black or white. They deal in absolutes and believe everything is either right or wrong. They believe in stability, steadiness and conformity. They believe there is only one way to do something and it is either right or wrong.

5. *Diversity and Achievement* — This group grows spiritually when they are allowed to do things many different ways. They are eager to change in the interest of finding a better way. They like new songs and freedom to innovate many changes in a local church.

6. *Relationships and Acceptance* — This group is people centered and they like close bonds of intimacy with other members. They like to have a close support system for each other. They like family closeness and are very sensitive to the needs of other members. They are very grace oriented and like to provide healing to those who have been beaten down by the rules.

> It is imperative that the praying servant leader love all of these people in these groups, in all their diversity.

7. *Adaptability* — This group is ready to change. They don't get locked into certain ways of doing things unless the Bible says that is the only way to do it. They don't force people to conform to their changes, but they do believe in change when circumstances demonstrate a need for it. They thrive on education, research and much information to provide ways to change and better adapt to people's needs.

8. *World Community* — This group does not want to be judgmental about any religious group. They will work with everything good in a community which will

Ask yourself: Is your congregation communicating only in ways that appeal to a few of these thinking systems? What can you do to change this situation?

help it develop spiritually or improve community morals.

It is imperative that the servant leader love all of these people in these groups. It seems impossible because there is such diversity. However, love and servanthood can be the spiritual bond to mold these groups into a volunteer army marching the same direction for Jesus Christ. It is not an easy task.

Be honest: Are you an agent for bringing unity in diversity to your congregation?

As church leaders we need to meet the basic needs found in these eight groups and take these people from where they are to where God wants them to be.

The biggest movement in the education world as we enter the third millennium is the multiple intelligences movement. It points out the uniqueness and diversity of people. People don't have one IQ, but they have

> We are not stuck with the intelligence level with which we are born.

eight IQs—in eight different areas. Intelligence is not fixed. We are not stuck with the intelligence level with which we are born. We have the ability to develop this intellectual capacity. Each of the eight different intelligences must include:

1. Skills enabling individuals to resolve genuine problems.
2. The ability to create an effective ministry or product.
3. The potential for identifying problems so solutions can be found to the problems.

A thumbnail sketch of the 8 intelligences includes:

1. Verbal/Linguistic — these people learn primarily from words and language. They like to read and listen. They also like to write and speak. This intelligence has dominated the educational system of the United States as well as most churches.
2. Logical/Mathematical — Often called scientific thinking, this intelligence deals with inductive and deductive thinking. They are interested in reasoning, numbers and the recognition of abstract pat-

Points to ponder: How do you learn best? Are you able to see how others fit better in other learning environments? Are your classes structured to help *all* learners?

terns. They like to analyze data and brainstorm ideas. They are left-brained and like to organize classes, lessons and services in logical ways.

3. Visual/Spatial — these people are visual and have the ability like an architect to visualize what an auditorium or office should look like. They have the ability to visualize an object along with the ability to create internal mental images and pictures.

4. Bodily/Kinesthetic — these people learn by doing and enjoy physical movement. They learn from acting and drama. They like to build models, visit people, and get involved in active projects.

5. Musical/Rhythmic — they like to put things together by rhythm and beat. They are like a symphony conductor putting everything together. They would like to learn the books of the Bible by singing them. They love music and rhythm. They may be able to play songs without knowing notes.

6. Naturalist — recognizes and appreciates nature and the natural world. They want us to leave the environment alone or protect it because they enjoy nature. They would like aquariums and plants in the classrooms and foyers.

> Prayer is moving from worshiping at my own golden altar to God's wash basin and towel.

7. Interpersonal — these people learn by working together. They thrive on relationships and team projects. They rely on others and pull ideas out of others. They believe teamwork is the name of the game. They like to tutor one another and solve problems as a team.

8. Intrapersonal — This group tends to be more private. They like to reflect and meditate. They think about and process feelings and emotions. They keep a personal "to do" list, make their action plan, prioritize items and set goals. Sometimes they are

thinking about what needs to be done to survive. At other times, they are reflecting on ways to go to the top.

These eight intelligences have a powerful message for the church in the third millennium. We must make biblical changes which meet the needs of all the people. A church assembly or classroom can no longer be a place where people just sit down and listen. We are in the multiintelligence, multisensory age, and we must use everything at our disposal to teach and communicate. Videos, computers, multisensory presentations and participatory classes and services will become more important each year.

More information about Multiple Intelligences can be obtained from:

Kagan Cooperative Learning
1160 Calle Cordillera
San Clemente, CA 92673

Now, let's take this chapter to a higher level and look at the correlation between Systems Analysis, Multiple Intelligences, and Spiritual Gifts:

Systems Analysis	*Multiple Intelligence*	*Spiritual Gifts*
Survival	**Intrapersonal** (Self Smart)	**Mercy Show-er**
Many problems living one day at a time and trying to survive.	Reflects on emotions and feelings, thinks about what needs to be done to survive as well as reach the top.	Shows empathy and compassion for those with problems, a feeler.
Safety	**Naturalist** (Nature Smart)	**Prophet**
Doesn't want things changed. Wants to be part of something that's predictable and feels safe.	Don't change the world or environment. I want to learn from it and enjoy it.	Points out wrongs in world. Tends to be traditional. Keep things black and white.
Strength and Power	**Logical/Mathematical** (Logic Smart)	**Givers**
Not great team player. Wants services, classes and programs to meet his needs. Will follow strong leadership.	Can give logical reasons for doing things the way he wants it.	It's not logical to him why people don't give more to make a difference. Realizes there can be strength and power tied to money.
Truth	**Logical/Mathematical** (Logic Smart)	**Evangelist**
Deals in absolutes, everything is either right or wrong. Likes stability.	Can give logical reasons for why something is either right or wrong.	Wants to teach the truth of the gospel.

Diversity and Achievement
Grows spiritually when allowed to do things many different ways. Likes new songs and freedom to innovate many changes in the church.

Relationships and Acceptance
People centered, likes close relationships. Grace oriented, provides healing for those who have been beaten down.

Adaptability
Constantly ready to change, not locked into certain way of doing things. Change based on research.

Adaptability
Constantly ready to change. Change can be based on what's practical space-wise.

World Community
Does not want to be judgmental about any religious group. Will work with anything good in a community which will help it develop spiritually or improve community morals.

Musical/Rhythmic (Music Smart)
Likes to put things together many different ways to have a peak experience — like a symphony conductor putting everything together.

Interpersonal (People Smart)
Emphasizes relationships. Loves to work with other people and form close relationships.

Verbal/Linguistic (Word Smart)
Learns from reading and research. Knowledge explosion, causing great change in today's world.

Verbal/Spatial (Space Smart)
Ability to visualize how church should be to effect change.

Body/Kinesthetic (Body Smart)
Learns by doing and being active. Likes to take things apart and fix anything that needs fixing. Likes to build a model for a better world or environment.

Exhorter
Encourages everyone with all their different gifts to work together in harmony.

Pastor
Shepherd wants close relationship with the flock.

Teacher
Encourages in-depth study to learn what to do.

Administration
Adapting to everything that will help a church function more efficiently and effectively.

Server
Helps any way he can for any good cause.

For your consideration: Can you see how this analysis of the physical feeding of the crowd applies to spiritual feeding of God's flock?

Now, let's apply all of these principles to the feeding of the 5,000 in Mark 6:30-44. It will take a while to get used to this style of teaching using the eight thinking systems, eight multiple intelligences and spiritual gifts. But it will give you new insights and help you reach people with whom you have never connected before. This has the possibility of revolutionizing our Bible school curriculum in the third millennium. It will also enable us to make needed changes in our assemblies, Bible classes, small groups and ministries to better meet the needs of others. Jesus never said it would be easy, but we need to use every available means in every available way to meet the needs of people so they can be all Jesus wants them to be.

138

Feeding of the 5,000
Mark 6:30-44

Teacher's Objective: *Jesus can use you to meet the needs of others.*

1. Reporting — v. 30 "apostles gathered around Jesus and reported to him all they had done and taught.

Adaptability	Verbal/Linguistic	Teacher
to research/share results of mission trip (Reports were different as they adapted to each situation.)	*word and language reporting*	*in-depth report*

   ✧ Share in groups what they had taught.
   ✧ Write a newspaper story of what they had done and taught.
   ✧ Share a TV news broadcast of what the apostles had done and taught.

2. Rest and Reflection — v. 31 "Come with me by yourselves to a quiet place and get some rest."

Survival	Intrapersonal	Mercy Show-er
tired, rest, trip over, crowd all around	*reflect, meditate*	*empathetic — need for rest*

   ✧ What did they reflect on during their quiet time?
   ✧ Write a poem or draw a picture of their feelings.

3. Compassion — v. 34 "When Jesus . . . saw a large crowd, he had compassion on them."

Relationships and Acceptance	Interpersonal	Pastor
saw needs	*related to them personally*	*loving shepherd for sheep*

   ✧ Hold up a shoe and ask the class to write a paragraph or share in groups what it's like to be a sheep without a shepherd.

4. Can't help them with food — v. 36 "Send the people away so they can . . . buy themselves something to eat."

Safety	Naturalist	Prophet
Don't change things, not my responsibility	*world & neighborhood same, will provide so can take care of selves*	*report what's wrong, no food, let them get it*

   ✧ What kind of food would they buy? What would it look like, smell like, and taste like?

5. Feed the people — v. 37 Jesus said, "You give them something to eat."

Strength and Power	Logical/Mathematical	Givers
primarily interested in self, follow strong leadership, strength in numbers	*count how many needed to be fed, how to do it*	*want to give enough to help*

✧ Prepare a menu and grocery list for 5,000 men.
✧ What are the main foods you would feed them?
✧ How much would it cost today?
✧ How long would it take to get it ready?

6. Search the crowd for food — v. 38 "found . . . 'five [loaves] — and two fish.'"

World Community	Body/Kinesthetic	Server
everybody	*learn by doing*	*just help*

✧ How long did it take for them to search the crowd to find this?
✧ Pantomime going through the crowd and looking for food.

7. Groups — v. 39 "Have all the people sit down in groups on the green grass."

Adaptability	Visual/Spatial	Administration
to situation	*see how groups can be arranged*	*organize this*

✧ Draw a diagram on a sheet of paper of how you would have arranged the 5,000 men.

8. The Blessing — v. 41 Jesus blessed the food and the disciples set it before the people.

Diversity and Achievement	Musical/Rhythmic	Exhorter
lots of ways to do this	*upbeat words of blessing & gratitude*	*encourager*

✧ What song of gratitude might the people sing?
✧ Hum a song that expresses your feelings when you are happy and grateful.

9. Needs Met — v. 42 "They all ate and were satisfied."

Truth	Logical/Mathematical	Evangelist
fact	*all fed*	*more receptive to truth*

✧ Share in groups why these 5,000 men would now be more receptive to the gospel.
✧ Reflect and write down on paper the number of opportunities you had this past week to help someone who was not a Christian.
✧ Prepare a lesson outline to teach these 5,000 men how to become Christians.

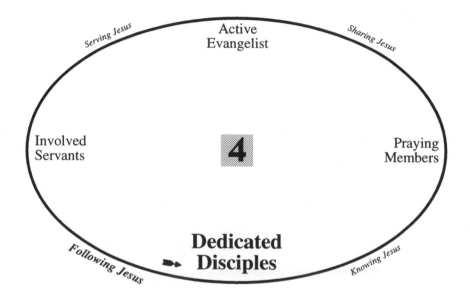

We're three quarters of the way around the track. For the first quarter we stressed the importance of **Praying Members** knowing Jesus. We then followed the biblical model from the book of Acts as these Praying Members became **Active Evangelists** sharing Jesus. We just concluded the third quarter of the race where members become **Involved Servants** serving Jesus. Now, we are ready for the final quarter of the race. We must produce **Dedicated Disciples** who truly follow Jesus. A disciple is a learner and dedicated follower of Jesus. We must strive to reach this level of maturity and commitment.

Prayer Produces a Shepherding Plan

There are some fundamental expectations for dedicated disciples:

1. People should know they are disciples because of their great love for other brothers and sisters in Christ.
2. They should be regular exhorters and encouragers in our assemblies.
3. They should be daily students of the word of God and regular attenders of Bible classes offered.
4. They should be committed to prayer.
5. They should be tithers.
6. They should be involved in a small group.
7. They should be mentors and have mentors.
8. They should have prayer partners.
9. They should be active evangelists as those in the early church were told to make disciples of all nations.
10. They should develop their leadership potential.
11. They should be involved in ministry.
12. They should hunger for the meat of the word.
13. They should develop their spiritual gifts to their greatest potential.
14. They should be prayer servants.

Dedicated disciples should also have five assurances:

1. The assurance of God's grace and their own salvation.

A bit of self-evaluation: How do you measure up to this checklist for dedication?

Prayer is fixing my heart and mind on Christ.

2. The assurance of answered prayer.
3. The assurance of victory over temptations.
4. The assurance of forgiveness.
5. The assurance of God's guidance and wisdom.

Their daily living should demonstrate:

1. They put Christ first every day.
2. They depend on the strength of Jesus Christ, and to Him belongs the glory.
3. They depend on the word of God for daily guidance.
4. They daily apply Christ's great command to love one another.
5. They are learners about stewardship and regularly examine their attitudes about giving.
6. They demonstrate that the church is people and not a building. They are willing to give themselves for the needs of people because this is what Jesus did at the cross.
7. They do good works because their faith leads them to do this. They do not do it in an attempt to earn favor with God.
8. They communicate the gospel to others.

A church will never produce dedicated disciples unless it has dedicated church leaders who are role models. It will also probably not happen unless elders are fulfilling their primary role as shepherds. Let's look at a plan to shepherd every member.

Think about it: If you are reading this book and are Are you not an elder, let me encourage you to pray for presently praying regularly for your shepherds daily. Jeremiah 3:15 says: "I will give your shepherds? you shepherds after my own heart, who will lead you Will you? with knowledge and understanding."

> A church will never produce dedicated disciples unless it has dedicated church leaders.

I have never known of a great shepherding ministry to begin unless shepherds first pour their hearts out to God in prayer. They are overwhelmed with the needs and hurts in the church family. They are convicted that they truly need to be shepherds. Many have told me they spend more time in elders meetings than they do actually shepherding the flock. Their hearts are broken when they see the role for which God has called them. The job is overwhelming, and they cannot do it with their own might. But the Great Shepherd will strengthen them and provide them wisdom.

Shepherds need to make some major commitments to prayer on behalf of the church family. They need to pray by name for those people who are not attending regularly as well as those who are hurting. They should divide up their responsibilities and make a commitment to try to pray in every member's home within a calendar year. Prayer in every home is usually at the heart of every financial campaign. It can be of even greater importance for a shepherding ministry. When you have prayed in every member's home, you are in touch with the sheep. The sheep know you and you know them. You have sat where they sat and walked where they walked. This does wonders for shepherding.

> Many have told me they spend more time in elders meetings than they do actually shepherding the flock.

There are two kinds of shepherding:

1. Leadership shepherding — this provides ways for elders to communicate and encourage other church leaders. You cannot let this group get spiritually down. At the annual selection of deacons, elders should divide up their responsibilities and take their wives to pray in the home of every prospective deacon and his wife. This provides incredible spiritual power on an annual basis. Through spiritual clusters, shepherds can have their leadership group meet with them once a month in the elder's home. Prayer is also an important ingredient of this meeting as well as learning about any problems that need to be tended to. Shepherds can also send birthday cards, spiritual

145

Ponder this:
How do the
two areas of
shepherding
relate to each
other? Are your
shepherds
involved in
both ministries?

birthday cards, encouragement cards, prayer cards and wedding anniversary cards to people whose ministries are represented in their spiritual cluster.

2. Lost Sheep Shepherding — is developing and implementing a plan to follow up on absentees and struggling members, and preventing people from falling through the cracks. The greatest need I have heard from elders at hundreds of retreats which I have conducted is: WE MUST DEVELOP A PLAN TO SHEPHERD THE CONGREGATION.

Let's look at the steps of a plan that is simple, profound, and successful:

1. Divide up the inactive members so that elders are praying each week for every inactive and hurting person.
2. Commit to the congregation that an elder will be in EVERY home within a calendar year to pray with each family.
3. Practice leadership shepherding. The annual selection of deacons and ministry leaders allows you to pray in the home of every deacon with his wife. Use your spiritual clusters for leadership shepherding.
4. Develop a ministry plan whereby elders delegate out major ministry responsibilities to deacons and ministry leaders. More time has to be made available to the elders for shepherding.

Prayer is depending on God's grace to help others succeed where I have failed.

5. Develop Spiritual Clusters where each elder has an area of responsibility in shepherding with Adult Bible Classes, Ministries, Small Groups, and the congregation at large.
6. Develop a plan where you use the Adult Bible Class, Ministries, and Small Groups to shepherd. This can greatly reduce your shepherding load. Realistically — set a goal to have 75% of your

people in the Adult Bible Classes, 60% working in ministry, and 50% in small groups. If you shepherd through these three natural areas, the congregation at large will be of small enough size that you can shepherd it.

7. Develop a plan in the Adult Bible Class that is similar to this:

   A. Assign a shepherd to each class. The class will relate to him and share needs with him. They will also get to know the shepherd better and know whom to come to with problems.

   B. Develop a plan in class where every absentee is contacted by class members.

   C. Develop a team of people in class to help with class follow-up and undershepherding.

   D. The undershepherding team will let their shepherd know of individual problems. Use other ministries, ministers, counselors, and other elders to meet specific needs.

8. Develop a similar plan with small groups.

9. Develop a plan with the ministries.

   A. Each shepherd should have about a half dozen ministries in his spiritual clusters.

   B. Ministry leaders should meet one night a month in the shepherd's home for a spiritual clusters meeting.

   C. Every ministry should shepherd all the people involved in their ministry.

10. Now that we have used our Adult Bible Classes, small groups, and ministries for shepherding, it becomes manageable to shepherd the rest of the congregation.

   A. Divide the rest of the congregation into spiritual clusters with one shepherd to lead each cluster.

   B. Develop a team of undershepherds to shepherd with you in your cluster. Deacons and ministry leaders in your ministry clusters should especially serve with you as undershepherds.

Try it: Using the principles this book is laying out, work up a plan for your own class or classes. Bathe your planning in prayer.

147

C. Pray for every inactive member or hurting person.

D. Use the phone for quick contacts of absentees.

E. Visit those who are inactive.

F. Invite everybody in your cluster for a meal in your home at least once a year.

I like to name the Spiritual Clusters after the fruit of the spirit such as love, patience, faithfulness, etc. This encourages spiritual growth and dedicated disciples. Besides, new people are impressed and excited when they become a new member and you tell them they are part of the love spiritual cluster or the peace spiritual cluster.

It is also best to group the ministry clusters where they have some common needs and goals to meet and work closely together. Examples of this would be outreach, children, worship, family, youth, benevolence, etc.

An example of the complete shepherding plan would look something like illustration 8.

Try this exercise: List some reasons you have heard as to why people dropped out of attendance.

Although the majority of dropouts are caused by family problems or relational problems, the Adult Bible Class can be a useful tool in the prevention of dropouts. Shepherds are told to feed and tend the flock in Acts 20. Romans 10:17 says "Faith comes by hearing and hearing by the word of God." The word of God has power to build people to be dedicated disciples.

> We must accept people where they are and grow them to where he wants them to be.

But one word of caution. This is the last quarter of the race. We have a tendency to want all of our classes, small groups, services and ministries to be for mature disciples! We must accept people where they are and grow them to where he wants them to be. We must make sure our curriculum, services, groups, and ministries meet the needs of the Systems-Sensitive Groups, the Multiple Intelligences and the Spiritual Gifts. This is no easy accomplishment. The classes should also be used to

148

SHEPHERDING PLAN / PRAYER LIST

Foundations of Prayer

1. Pray by name for those hurting or inactive.
2. Pray in every home in your cluster.
3. Have every person in your cluster in your home for prayer and a meal.

Stapleton "LOVE" Outreach	Freeman "JOY" Children	Johnson "PEACE" Family
1. Baptismal Assistance	1. Bible Hour	1. Family Life Groups
2. Building Maintenance	2. Children's Singing & Drama	2. Adult Recreation
3. Family Care	3. Dorcas & Timothy	3. Young Couples
4. Building Directories	4. Education, Children	4. Grief Recovery
5. Ground Maintenance	5. Nursery & Child Care	5. Divorce Recovery
6. Adult Bible Class	6. Scouts	6. Support Groups
7. Small Groups	7. Jail & Prison	7. Parenting Support Groups
8. Congregation at Large	8. Mother's Day Out	8. Counseling — Volunteer
	9. Adult Bible Class	a. Prayer Warrior
	10. Small Groups	b. Mentor
	11. Congregation at Large	c. Listener
		d. Support Group Leader
		e. Trainer
		f. Volunteer Child Care
		9. Family Life Groups
		a. Host/Hostess
		b. Leader
		10. Adult Bible Class
		11. Small Groups
		12. Congregation at Large

Illustration 8a

Smith *"PATIENCE"* Missions	Noyes *"KINDNESS"* Benevolence	Rogers *"GOODNESS"* Youth
1. Missions	1. Community Care	1. Education, Youth
2. Church Growth	2. Contribution	2. Huddles
3. Sunshiners	3. Greeters	3. Youth
4. Community Outreach	4. Transportation	4. Finance
5. Ground Maintenance	5. High Plains Children's Home	5. Christian Camps & Retreats
6. Adult Bible Class	6. Meals on Wheels	6. Personal Finance
7. Small Groups	7. Parking	7. Adult Bible Class
8. Congregation at Large	8. Ushers	8. Small Groups
	9. Adult Bible Class	9. Congregation at Large
	10. Small Groups	
	11. Congregation at Large	

Illustration 8b

Thomas "FAITHFULNESS" Assemblies	Burns "GENTLENESS" Involvement	Wood "SELF-CONTROL" Adult Education
1. Hall Monitors	1. Involvement	1. Education
2. Lighting & Sound	2. New Member Assimilation	2. Library
3. Lord's Table Service	3. Calling & Caring	3. Women's Ministry
4. Prayer	4. Communication	4. Wedding Ministry
5. Tape	5. Visitation	5. Music Ministry
6. Information & Assistance	6. Hospital Visitation	6. Media
7. Adult Bible Class	7. Church Directories	7. Singles & College Program
8. Small Groups	8. Fellowship Dinners	8. Adult Bible Class
9. Congregation at Large	9. Office Volunteers	9. Small Groups
	10. Publicity & Promotion	10. Congregation at Large
	11. Special Events	
	12. Visitation — Shut-ins	
	13. Welcome Home	
	14. Wednesday Night Meals	
	15. Adult Bible Class	
	16. Small Groups	
	17. Congregation at Large	

Illustration 8c

Consider:
What do you
see as the
purpose for the
adult education
program? Is
your present
setup meeting
that purpose?

teach basic Bible knowledge, develop Christlike attitudes, and motivate people to be active in ministry. The Adult Bible Classes should also be used to mold every person to be a Praying Member, Active Evangelist, Involved Servant and Dedicated Disciple. The curriculum should include accomplishing these goals for every teaching program that involves adults. This includes: Sunday and Wednesday Bible Classes, worship services, Vacation Bible School, Small Groups, Family Life Groups, training programs, retreats and seminars, Ladies Classes, Sunday night classes, etc.

The loosely structured plan would include the following Bible Study Courses in a five-year plan. In addition to these basic Bible study courses, many topical studies and special courses need to be added to the curriculum to meet the needs of the different Systems-Sensitive Groups, Multiple Intelligences Groups, and Spiritual Gifts Groups.

Courses and training would also need to be added for new members, evangelistic training, ministry training and intensive discipleship courses. The five-year plan might look something like this:

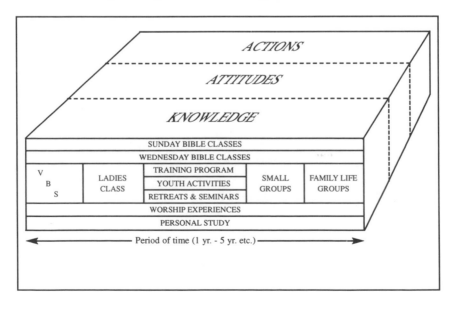

152

BIBLE STUDY COURSES — SIX MONTHS EACH

1. 1 & 2 THESSALONIANS, 1 & 2 TIMOTHY, TITUS, PHILEMON
2. CURRENT BIBLE-RELATED TOPICS AND ISSUES
3. LIFE OF CHRIST
4. GENESIS
5. EXODUS, JOSHUA, JUDGES, 1 & 2 SAMUEL, 1 & 2 KINGS
6. LESSONS IN CHRISTIAN LIVING
7. GALATIANS, EPHESIANS, PHILIPPIANS, COLOSSIANS
8. JAMES, 1 & 2 PETER, 1, 2, & 3 JOHN, JUDE
9. TRAINING AND EQUIPPING CLASSES
10. ACTS OF THE APOSTLES
11. ROMANS
12. 1 & 2 CORINTHIANS
13. REVELATION
14. OLD TESTAMENT SURVEY
15. HEBREWS
16. NEW TESTAMENT SURVEY

ADULT #1	18-30	1	2	3	4	5	6	7	8	9	10	11	12	13
ADULT #2	20-30	2	3	4	5	6	7	8	9	10	11	12	13	14
ADULT #3	30-40	3	4	5	6	7	8	9	10	11	12	13	14	15
ADULT #4	40-50	4	5	6	7	8	9	10	11	12	13	14	15	16
ADULT #5	50-60	5	6	7	8	9	10	11	12	13	14	15	16	1
ADULT #6	60 UP	6	7	8	9	10	11	12	13	14	15	16	1	2

The first rectangular block shows a plan to try to accomplish our goals for the adults. We are trying to develop a total teaching plan to accomplish these goals. On the next list are some of the suggested six-month curriculum courses. Each course has a number by the side of it. The next chart is filled with numbers and each number indicates a course. The chart shows how all of these courses can be taught in a five-year period of time. For example for the first six months:

Do this: Use the plan included here as a *general pattern* for devising your own plan.

　　Adult class #1 would be studying Thessalonians, Timothy, Titus, and Philemon

　　Adult class #2 would have Current Bible-Related Topics and Issues

Adult class #3 would be studying the Life of Christ

Adult class #4 would have Genesis

Adult class #5 would study Exodus through Kings

Adult class #6 would study Lessons in Christian Living

Now, look on the numbers chart and notice the classes for the next six months:

Adult class #1 would have Current Bible-Related Topics and Issues

Adult class #2 would be studying the Life of Christ

Adult class #3 would have Genesis

Adult class #4 would study Exodus through Kings

Adult class #5 would study Lessons in Christian Living.

Adult class #6 would go down to #7 Galatians through Colossians.

Prayer Produces Joyful Disciples

When Paul was talking about character, discipleship, and Christian maturity, he talked about the fruit of the Spirit. He listed *joy* as one of the nine characteristics of the fruit of the Spirit. When Jesus preached his greatest sermon, the Sermon on the Mount in Matthew 5, he told us that those who modeled those great disciple qualities which he described would be blessed or *happy*. I'm convinced the church needs more laughter, joy, celebration, and happiness in the third millennium. I'm tired of the world thinking of Christians as being unhappy people with sour, critical dispositions. If anyone has the right to truly be happy on this earth, it's a Christian. If you are tired, frustrated, hurting and nearly burned out, I hope you will learn to laugh again.

Be truly honest about this: Do your worship services encourage laughter and joy?

Some people suffer from terminal seriousness. No one should think they are so important or righteous that they can't laugh at their own foibles. There is no doubt that God has a wonderful sense of humor. After all, humor was his idea! When embarrassing things happen to us, we should hear God laughing and laugh along. None of us are immune to mistakes. Just as we laugh at our children's funny remarks — funny because they don't yet have an adult understanding of the situation — so God must have great fun laughing at us. These are funny things that have happened in the life of my wife and me along with our four children. The Fulenwider Family has had many burdens and struggles — but through it all there was always

> I'm tired of the world thinking of Christians as being unhappy people with sour, critical dispositions.

laughter along with the tears. Here are some funny things that happened to us on the way to heaven. May all of us learn to relax and laugh at ourselves.

COURTSHIP AND MARRIAGE

God prepared Ann and me for marriage to one another in very unusual ways. God knew I needed her so it must have been destiny. Ann was reared at Tipton Children's Home in Oklahoma and I attended the second through the twelfth grades in Childress, Texas. I played basketball, and we were invited to a tournament at Tipton for those who weighed 100 lbs. or less. I had never weighed over 100 lbs. in my life, but when I climbed on the scales at Tipton, they registered 102! Coach Dick Risenhoover had a solution. He had me put on heavy sweat clothes and run for the next 15 minutes around the gym before the game started. It worked! I climbed on the scales and weighed 100 lbs. But, my legs felt like rubber. I "jumped center" for us and fell on my face as the game began. I fell two or three more times running up and down the court, and the coach had to take me out as everyone was laughing at me. Seated in the stands laughing at this pudgy basketball player was my future wife! She never forgot that moment.

Does this story remind you of anything in your own life?

Our next meeting was at the Kirkland Church of Christ. Ann was an outstanding singer and sang in the Tipton Home Sextet. They came to sing at the Kirkland Church of Christ. The elders asked me to direct the chorus for one song and I really messed that up because I didn't know much music. But, I was 16 years old and had discovered girls. I asked one of the girls (not Ann) if I could take her to get a soda. The chorus director said it would be okay if I would hurry back. The store was only three blocks away, but I was just learning to drive. We got a soda quickly, but the car was a stick shift, and I could not get it in reverse. I tried for nearly an hour to get the car out of that situation. I finally revved the motor up as high as it would go, jumped over the high curb,

156

and drove the car down the sidewalk to the Tipton Home Bus at church. Ann and the other girls were sweltering in the heat on the bus and glaring at me! My "date" was scared to death and ran to board the bus in record time.

Our third significant meeting was while we were at Abilene Christian College. I didn't think I would ever get her to go out with me! I told her I thought there would be a strawberry milkshake for her at a table in a park. I'd had a friend put the milkshake there, and he had climbed up a tree to watch. When we arrived in the park, there was the milkshake on the table. But Ann was afraid in the darkness of the park, and there was a loud noise in the darkness as my friend had fallen out of the tree. Ann insisted we get out of there immediately, and she wouldn't even take the milkshake! My friend has become Dr. Willie Wilson, an elder in the church at Philadelphia!

I preached every Sunday while I was in college, and I was called before the men at a Men's Business Meeting with a complaint against me. They said: "Ray, you're okay as a preacher, but you make a horrible mess filling those communion cups each Sunday. Can you get someone to come with you and do this?" Abilene Christian had a rule that a girl could not go out of town with a boy when he preached unless the couple was engaged. So Ann and I had to be "engaged" on Sundays as she did an incredible job filling the communion cups and teaching the small children.

In God's timing, Ann and I were married December 21, 1963, in Childress, Texas, at the Church of Christ. Some of the guys tried to kidnap me after the wedding. Ann bit one of them so hard that his arm got infected and he had to go to the doctor for treatment! He is an elder at a church in Dallas today.

We got married in a 12-inch snowstorm, and it took us four hours to drive 30 miles to Quanah, Texas, where the roads were blocked. We had not planned to spend our wedding night in Quanah, but we got the last room at an 80-year-old hotel where it was so cold a glass of water froze inside the room. The bathtub was so tall it nearly came to Ann's chin. Cost per night was a whopping $4! We went to church in Quanah the next morning. We told the people we spent the night at the Quanah Hotel together. People really looked at us strange because I signed the guest register at church as Ray Fulenwider and my wife signed her maiden name, Ann Hampton! I was also hurt when my wife described me in a letter to a friend after the honeymoon as the missing link between man and monkey because I was so hairy!

EATING MEALS WITH THE BRETHREN

Eating can be an usual experience for a preacher. We've sat on milk cans and eaten jumping frog legs and rattlesnake! We've had the cows chew the paint off the car while we were eating. And we've learned not to "make love" after eating Texas jalapeños!

HOME REPAIRMEN

What's the worst handyman disaster you ever had?

I've never been much of a repairman. In fact, I even have trouble changing a lightbulb. My first night at Lubbock after I had just accepted a job with the Broadway Church of Christ is one I will always remember. The kitchen faucet was leaking, so I started working on it around midnight. I got water shooting up to the ceiling! I looked in the Broadway Church Directory and called the deacon in charge of building maintenance around 1:00 a.m. He came over and took care of the problem, but I really got off to a bad start with him.

About the same thing happened, when we came to Amarillo. However, this deacon told me to just turn the water off for the night. I couldn't get the water off as I learned later I was turning off the sprinkler system! He finally came over and turned it off.

BABY-SITTING THE CHILDREN

Baby-sitting with my children when they were

young was usually exciting for me. Once when I was counseling a lady on the phone and baby-sitting three-year-old Deana, she came to me with a stomachache. I told her to wait a few minutes and I would get her some infantol pink. Independent Deana went to the bathroom, climbed up the ledge and drank a whole bottle of infantol pink! I rushed her to the emergency room and had to get her stomach pumped!

A few years later I was baby-sitting Jeana and she drank a bottle of shampoo and half a bottle of mouthwash. That brought about another trip to the emergency room and another stomach pumping!

BIBLE SCHOOL SINGING

Our children have always kept us young at heart. I'll never forget Deana coming in from Ron Bailey's Bible Class singing: "He invites us into his baked potato and his banana over us is love!" That was before Veggie Tales!

AGING DAD IN SON'S EYES

There was the time that I took my son Joel with me on one of my speaking trips, and he told the elders I was his granddad! The elder introduced me to the congregation and told them he was glad I had brought my grandson with me!

BAPTIZING THE CAT

When Deana was six years old, she heard a tremendous lesson on baptism. She knew it was important, and she wanted everyone to be baptized. This included the family cat! However, she couldn't find enough water to baptize the cat. So she baptized the cat in an oil bucket, and the cat nearly died!

WHERE IS GOD?

Deana was with me on one of my speaking trips to Highland Church of Christ in Abilene. It was her first

What are the best "zingers" out of your children's mouths?

159

time to fly. I'll never forget her looking out the window that night and saying: "Dad, where is God?"

THE DAMAGED PAINTING

Joel and Jeana were once playing with a ping pong ball and our best painting got a deep thud in it. Ann thought Joel did it and spanked him. Jeana was the "perfect kid" who never got into trouble. Several years later at Christmas time, Jeana said that she had a confession to make. It was she and not Joel who had put the dent in the painting!

DEANA'S DATING

Deana had a lot of trouble dating when she was a teenager. Joel would always throw firecrackers on her dates from his upstairs window. Deana would also sometimes awaken the entire family when she leaned against the doorbell unknowingly during her good night kiss!

Deana's first real date was the climbing of Half Dome at Yosemite National Park. The date was with a Lubbock Christian College student during the Yosemite Encampment. The date lasted nine hours and when they got down from the mountain, his enduring words to her were: "You sure do sweat a lot!"

WRONG FLIGHT TIME

Jana worked one summer at Camp Shiloh in New York with inner-city students. She had told me she had to leave by plane at 6:00 a.m. on Sunday morning. We got up at 4:00 a.m., got ready, and rushed to the airport. The person at the ticket counter asked: "Have you changed your ticket?" Jana said: "No". He said: "Your ticket is for 6:00 a.m. on Monday morning!"

VAN TRAVEL

Travel has always been interesting in the Fulenwider family. We've had the girls' makeup mirrors catch the van on fire because of the sun shining on them.

And we've had the messy port-a-potty fall out of the van in some of the worst places and circumstances.

MY FIRST FLIGHT

I'll never forget my first flight. I was 25 years old, and the flight was from Dallas to New York City. It took me three hours to get to New York City and three hours to get out of the airport! I had been told to pick up the red phone at the airport when I arrived and call limousine service. I did this every 15 minutes for the next three hours!

Finally, the man on the red phone said, "Where are you? We've been looking for you for hours?" I said, "I'm right here by this red telephone!" He said, "There are over 100 red phones in this airport! You are supposed to go to the transportation pickup area on the north side of the building!"

THE TIRE-SMOKED STEAKS

Ann and I have always had a gift to attract a community's attention. Dr. C.L. Kay was a dignitary whom we invited to speak at Rule High School when I was a school principal. We wanted to make a good impression on Dr. Kay, so we decided to charcoal some steaks for his meal. But a snowstorm came up! I was determined to have some charcoal steaks for Dr. Kay, so I moved the charcoal grill into the garage. The grill caught several tires on fire in the garage rafters! I have never seen so much smoke in my life! Someone called the fire department. When Dr. Kay arrived, the fire department was spraying water all over the garage! The steaks were ruined and it was quite an embarrassing moment.

Have you had attempts to impress others backfire on you?

WASHING THE CAR

A few months later Ann stuck the car in the front yard while she was washing it. I think half the community must have been there to see the tow truck pull our car out of the front yard grass!

161

WORSHIP SERVICES

Do this:
Start writing down all the humorous, embarrassing, even ridiculous things that have happened to you and your family inside and outside the assembly. Then thank God for keeping you humble!

Some of our funniest experiences have happened during worship services. God must really have a sense of humor. We had four people come forward on Sunday morning at Richland Hills to be baptized, but the water in the baptistery was boiling! The youth had had a lock-in over the weekend and turned the thermostat as high as it would go! Believing in the importance of baptism, I organized some of the deacons to get huge trash barrels, run to the kitchen ice machine and fill the trash containers with ice. Each time we poured a bucket of ice in the baptistery, there was so much "smoke" or steam rising, it looked like the Holy Spirit ascending! Finally, after about fifteen minutes of dumping many barrels of ice into the baptistery, we got the water cool enough to baptize the four people.

Then there was the time that a minister from a neighboring congregation and his wife responded to the invitation in Benjamin, Texas. They had been having some marital problems and were crying. Ann and I were not married at the time, but she was with me on one of our "engaged Sundays." Anyway, the couple who had responded were standing up front as they hugged and cried. She took out my lapel handkerchief, and I have never seen such a shocked look on a respondent! Ann had blotted my handkerchief with her lipstick, and this girl was staring at the big red blotch as she held the handkerchief up at an angle where all of the congregation could see the lipstick on the handkerchief. I think Ann ducked under a seat, and I felt like requesting prayers myself! I finally led a prayer for them up front. That couple is happily married today, and he is an elder in the church.

I once moved Sunday night services to the lake in Abilene. I wanted to be just like Jesus and preach from a boat on the water. We had a large crowd, and everything worked fine until the blowing wind started rocking the boat. I preached about a two-minute sermon and spent the rest of the time "upchucking" over the side of the boat!

One of my thrills in life was taking my entire family to Yosemite National Encampment. I was told I would be speaking to over 10,000 people at once! About ten minutes into my lesson, I swallowed a gnat in this open air setting. I tried everything I knew, but I could not clear my throat. It was over! On the trip back to Texas in the blue van, I asked the "kids" what they enjoyed most about Yosemite. They said it was seeing me swallow the gnat, and my expressions that followed as I tried to speak!

I preached an unusual sermon once in Rockport, Texas. We were on vacation and drove into Rockport around 5:30 p.m. on Sunday. I had on a new, blue jumpsuit and ran to the dock to fish for a few minutes when we arrived. I knew time would be short because we would be going to church services at 6:00 p.m. I caught a big fish, but lo and behold, I ripped a big hole in the seat of my jumpsuit when I caught the fish! There was a nail sticking out of the dock where I was sitting. My aunt, uncle, and Ann were with me on this trip. They rushed out of the cabin and said we were late for church. I jumped in the car and did not tell them anything about my ripped jumpsuit! We slipped into the back row at church and were about ten minutes late. I don't know how anyone knew I was going to be there, but the preacher got up and said he was so glad Ray Fulenwider was in the audience, and they would like for him to preach tonight! My uncle had a suit coat and tie on — and they thought he was me! They came up behind him — he sputtered and said he had never preached and pointed to me! I walked up to the pulpit with my back to the wall as much as possible. It was so good to get behind the pulpit. I didn't know what to do when the sermon was over. During the invitation song, I kept standing behind the safety of the pulpit and three people came forward! I kept standing behind the pulpit! The preacher baptized the three people who responded as I stayed behind the pulpit. The people never did know why I stayed behind the pulpit for such a long period of time!

11 Prayer Produces Good Changes

"Put God in charge of your work, then what you've planned will take place" (Prov. 16:3, *The Message*).

Be honest: How do you respond when your leadership begins talking about change?

This chapter wasn't originally planned for this book. I wrote a lengthy chapter in *The Servant-Driven Church* entitled "The Servant's Way to Manage Conflict and Change." But good change is so important for the new millennium, I must write this chapter. It will be short, but it is so important. My prayer is that it will be used by many church leaders all over the world to bring about good change.

A BLUEPRINT FOR CHANGE

We will follow an acrostic to simplify the material. Change comes when there is:

C ause for unhappiness

H ard work

A new vision

N ew plans with a good chance for success

G ood communication

E veryone prays

Let's look at these powerful change agents individually:

1. Cause for unhappiness

Many innovative church leaders have failed to understand this, but change will not take place unless the leaders and the people are dissatisfied. This is a difficult point because dissatisfaction can be a perception, and it can be manipulated. Nonetheless, change will not take place unless there is unhappiness with the present situation. People may be dissatisfied with lack of spiritual maturity, lack of evangelism, losing the young people, broken homes, needs not being met, etc. We need to find out why people are unhappy. And church leaders need to team up with the congregation to determine what can be done to improve the situation. It can be a win-win scenario. An example might be a group of young couples who are unhappy because there is no Children's Bible Hour during the service. They meet with the church leaders, share the need, and good change takes place. Maybe there is an elderly group who do not come to services after the sun goes down. They meet with the church leaders and ask for an earlier meeting time and good change takes place. Many people might be unhappy with the "worship songs" and "worship services" so changes with options might need to be made.

> Change will not take place unless the leaders and the people are dissatisfied.

2. Hard work.

It's always easier to not rock the boat. The energy required for change is hard work. It requires gathering a lot of input from the congregation. Some are locked into certain traditions and believe change will threaten their values. It is hard work to gather information, listen to complaints, meet with people, and try to do what's best. This is where we really need hard-working church leaders who will not try to take shortcuts. It's hard work to read a lot of books, attend seminars and workshops, use e-mail and computer programs, look at videos, visit other places, and strive to be the church leader God needs. Always remember that if it were easy, anybody could do it! But God has called leaders after his own heart for "such a time as this."

3. A new vision.

There must be a new vision for the congregation. It should reinforce the vision statement of the congregation. It should address the needs and the complaints. People should feel this is God's idea and God's vision for the church. They need to be sold on a higher calling to serve Him. They must see higher values and better

Consider carefully: Do you have a clear idea of where your congregation needs to be going?

church life. People are fed up with mediocrity. People should be motivated by a vision which they feel they have been called together by God to implement. Church leaders should be united in this new vision.

4. New plan with a good chance of success.

Input needs to be obtained from every member. There must be ownership by everyone for the new plan. Complaints from negative people must be overcome. Praying with them and listening to them can produce great results. Having people on opposite ends of the spectrum meet together can produce great results. It's always good to begin these meetings with a season of prayer. Then ask each person to empty his spiritual cup and suggest ideas that would be best to meet the needs of everyone in the church. Each person needs to totally deny himself, and ask what Jesus would do in each situation. Thank the people for coming and conclude with a season of prayer.

> The plan should enable people to know where we are going.

A plan by creditable people should be developed. It should make sense. The plan should help you reach your new vision. The plan should enable people to know where we are going. People hate surprises. The plan should be "bathed in prayer" and a plan developed for change where people will not have week-to-week surprises. Let people know early why you are doing what you are doing.

5. Good communication.

Think about it:
What happens if you don't communicate plans well enough? What can you do to improve communication?

This is so important. The best communication involves taking people from the known to the unknown and back to the known. If you are thinking about projecting songs on the screens in the auditorium, let people first see a demonstration of what it is like to do this. If they are asking about a power-point presentation in a Bible class — show them how the lesson comes from the Bible and the power-point presentation is like an outline on the screen. Share a demonstration of this so people can understand what's going on.

Good communication is imperative to keep our Values, Purpose, and Mission Statements before the congregation. People should know what will never change as far as our values are concerned, and this will provide them with a comfort zone. They should know where the church is trying to go and why. They should know who we are, whose we are, and where we are going. Communication also includes openness and meeting with people who have questions about what's happening. Listening and prayer time is very important.

The ability to take criticism is also important. Church leaders cannot please everyone. Develop the best two-way communication program you can and build a church that best exemplifies what Jesus Christ would have you do.

> The best communication involves taking people from the known to the unknown and back to the known.

Again, I repeat — no surprises! Please communicate what is going to happen and why before it happens. Take time to teach God's word about change and what you are doing BEFORE it happens!

6. Everyone pray

Develop prayer guides and prayer emphasis programs where people are praying about the values, mission, and purpose of the church. Have them praying about the new vision and new plans for the church. Have them pray for a church that will be all God wants it to be. Have them pray for a revival for the church. Have them pray that each person will be a praying servant doing exactly what Jesus would do. Have each member pray that the church leaders will be filled with power and wisdom to make needed changes.

Point to ponder: Is your church prayer-driven in everything you do — *especially* changes?

Church leaders — pray for God's wisdom for the right TIMING to make needed changes. The right timing is critical! Pray also for boldness and courage. Wrestle with God as Jacob wrestled with the angel. Don't dare let Satan or pressures keep you from making the changes Jesus would make in his Church!

12 Prayer Gets the Church Ready for the Future

"Jesus Christ is the same yesterday and today and forever" (Heb. 13:8).

As we look into the future, we need to remember that some things never change. Our major goal of making dedicated disciples has never changed. It was Jesus' last request to us in both Matthew 28:19-20 and Acts 1:8. It will be our goal throughout the ages. We need to produce disciples who are:

Dedicated
Involved
Servants
Christians
Innovative
Prayerful
Learners and Lovers
Evangelistic

Ask yourself:
Are *you* this kind of disciple? Are you doing your best to produce disciples in this pattern?

These **dedicated** disciples believe their main task in a church is to produce disciples who make other disciples. They model what they teach, and they do not take their tasks lightly. They are dedicated followers of Jesus Christ and are willing to do anything, anywhere, anytime for the cause of his church.

These disciples are **involved** in serving their Master. They are willing to "wash feet" or get their "hands dirty" for the cause of Christ. They model the fruit of the spirit and use their God-given gifts for the glory of God.

These disciples are unselfish **servants**. Things do not have to be done their way to please them. They want

168

things done God's way. They deny themselves and their desires to allow the church to use biblical methods that best serve the needs of the entire church and meet the needs of the unchurched. This is true spiritual maturity. They have learned that the greatest disciple is a servant.

> The greatest disciple is a servant.

These disciples are **Christians** who are radical followers of Jesus Christ. They want to follow him as their model. They put the cause of Christ above everything else, and this greatly alters their priorities and values.

These **innovative** disciples use every available means in every available way to reach every available soul. They "brainstorm" and get "outside the box." They are not afraid to dream. They are constantly looking for new ways to teach and demonstrate the same old gospel story.

These disciples are men and women of **prayer**. It is the single greatest driving force of their lives. They are people after God's own heart. They pray for God's wisdom and help before every task they attempt.

> The simplest definition of a disciple is that they are learners.

These disciples are **learners** and **lovers**. The simplest definition of a disciple is that they are learners. They want to learn more about Jesus and his church. They are committed to learning the word of God. They also love the body of Christ and the church. They know that the world knows they are disciples because of the love they have and demonstrate for their brothers and sisters in Christ.

Disciples must be **evangelistic**. They pray for the unchurched, and they share their story with the unchurched. They know that sharing their story in their own words is one of the most powerful ways to lead someone to Jesus Christ. They would never just be academic followers of Jesus Christ. They know they have received forgiveness and grace from Jesus Christ, and they want to produce other disciples for Him. They have a driving passion to fulfill this mission.

Before we look at the future, let's take a brief look at the different generations. When we understand each group and their needs, it will help us better understand our future journey.

FIVE GENERATIONS OF AMERICANS

Generation	Years of Birth	Age Range in 2000	Population Size
Seniors/Power Builders	1926 & earlier	74 and older	19.9 million
Builders/Peace Makers	1927-1945	55-73	39.8 million
Boomers/Path Finders	1946-1964	36-54	73.1 million
Busters/Pace Setters	1965-1983	17-35	72.2 million
Mosaics/Gen-X	1984-2002	16 & younger	61.7 million

Consider: Name someone you know who is a classic example of that generation acording to these definitions. How well do you fit the stereotype for your own generation?

The Seniors or Power Builders were born during 1901-1926. They represent around 20 million of our population. They have always had a great passion to learn and do not understand why motivation at church is so important to younger generations. The majority are left-brained rationalists who rely more on reason than multisensory perceptions to discover knowledge. They follow head more than heart. This practical generation is a problem-solving, analytical group. Just tell them what the problem is and they will solve it. They like things orderly and well organized. They like lecture, memorization and drill. They are active doers and financial givers. They like to sing old-time Christian hymns. They love to study the Bible and are not too interested in learning from videos, computer screens, and technology and e-mail. Duty drives them to be the Christians they should be. This generation was the builders of the great churches in America. This group is also known as the GI generation. They have a great instinct for survival. They survived World War I, the Great Depression and World War II. They are the grandparents of the Baby Boomers.

> Seniors have a great instinct for survival.

170

The Peace Makers or Builders were born during 1927-1945. They represent nearly 40 million people and are the parents of the Baby Boomers. They stress relationships over knowledge. They plead for the church members to get along with one another. They have a high tolerance level, and they like to include others in decision making. They like intergenerational Bible classes and like to do things with children. They are open to discussing new ideas, but they don't like for things to be left open-ended. They like for things to be planned and organized. They like highly organized job descriptions and organized class structures. They believe every church should have a five- or ten-year plan. They are very pragmatic and want the church to meet the needs of today's people. They like outlines and how-to-do books on church work. The Peace Makers are good facilitators. They learn more by ear than sight, but they are open to some other ways of learning. Many of these people love church music. The majority like a traditional service, but many of them desire a contemporary service. This generation is the consumer generation. They discovered time payments and mortgages. They led the U.S. to incredible economic and industrial expansion. They learned to make money and they learned to give. They are usually the major givers in the church.

Point for discussion: What are the strerghths and weaknesses of each generation?

The Baby Boomers or Path Finders were born during 1946-1964. This is the largest generation and

> Despite many problems, Baby Boomers have usually been very optimistic.

represents more than seventy-three million people. Despite many problems, this group has usually been very optimistic. This is the most educated generation in history, but they also value experience for learning. This is the first generation reared with many absentee fathers. This generation was reared in an affluent world and had television as a significant parenting tool.

This group is very idealistic. They want to change the world and the church, and they believe it can be done very simply. They are never quite satisfied spiritually, and they continually search for spiritual satisfaction. They view truth and values as absolute and fixed rather than relative and changing. They do not like for their values and ideas to be questioned. They search logically for truth in the word. This may be an end in itself for them. They are sometimes slow to get involved and implement things. They are more interested in what's best for them than they are interested in what's best for the entire church or the entire country. They desire great variety in class topics, learning styles, programs and songs. This generation demands a high quality religious education program for children. If you can get them to teach they do a great job, but they are more interested in teaching their children than other children. This generation is very, very visual and they like screens in the auditorium, power point, computers, overhead projectors, video projectors, etc.

The Baby Busters or Pace Setters were born from 1965-1983. There are over seventy-two million in this group. These are the children of the Baby Boomers. This generation tends to be very pessimistic and critical.

> Baby Busters are struggling for survival, and they want teaching that will help them get through this day or week.

Many feel that the church is not interested in their needs. They hate words like sanctification, justification, etc. They are not interested in theology, heaven, hell or the hereafter. They are interested in what works now. They like to learn truth from stories, Bible characters, and fellow strugglers. They are struggling for survival, and they want teaching that will help them get through this day or week. They are intense realists who rely on facts only. They reject the impractical, have trouble with faith, and doubt the visionary church leader. This generation desires love, attention, and direction. They are starved for relationships and attention. They are receptive to change if the Bible shows them they are wrong.

This generation is interested in studying what applies to every day life and working in ministries that make this happen. They sometimes struggle with the question: "Why do we need God?" All we need is the right education and we can accomplish anything. Why go to church? They believe it's more important for them to spend family time at home on Sunday night than it is for them to go to church. They like goals, mission, value, and purpose statements that are practical. They question the purpose of everything at church. They are not traditionalists. They want to know what the church is trying to accomplish and what is the purpose of each ministry.

This generation especially enjoys gender-based small group Bible study on a day or night of the week instead of on Sunday morning. Women especially like to study and pray with other women in a weekday small group.

> Prayer is not pushing the panic button when things seem out of control.

This generation likes to have an authentic group without prejudice. They like to worship with all the different racial groups present. They are tremendously upset with any negative remark made about another racial group, church, or religion.

Try this exercise: Design a Bible class and worship service to best meet the needs of each generation.

They like a lot of options, and they like for a lot of things to be going on at once. They view the worship service as a total experience to transform lives. They are reached more through the heart than the head. They truly represent the multisensory age and they grow from experiences using all eight learning intelligences.

Generation-X or the Mosaics are those born during 1984-2002. They will represent a large group of nearly sixty-two million people. Their characteristics are still emerging. This generation is in a world of incredible change and technology. They are highly educated and learn with all the multiintelligences. They cannot understand why there are many different churches, and many different religions. They want unity and believe Satan is winning the battle because of the disunity of religious people. This group likes informality and many options for services, classes, and programs. Prayer and faith are very important to them. They have grown up at a time of many broken homes, lowered moral ethics, alternate life styles, cohabitation before marriage, drug and alcohol abuse, violence, etc. They are trying to survive, but they have a drive that God can use to make this world and his church a better place.

This generation likes permission to put their faith and ideas into practice. They believe in great social programs, and they are frustrated if the church will not use them to feed the hungry and help the poor. They are starved for authentic, genuine people who really care about them and their needs.

This generation likes to praise God and sing and talk directly to him. They love to have their friends with them for these spiritual transforming experiences. They love to worship and study with all religious groups together. They are so committed they will attend group Bible studies or huge worship services together any night of the week. They like for this to be a joyful experience. They function best when things are chaotic, spontaneous and not tightly organized.

> Most declining churches are primarily meeting only the needs of those who are fifty-five years of age or older.

Most declining churches are primarily meeting only the needs of those who are fifty-five years of age or older. This only represents about twenty-two percent of the population and very few of them will be on this earth twenty years from now. Let's pray now that God will help us meet the needs of all the generations and lead them to be dedicated disciples for Jesus Christ.

And, now we come to the future and the new millennium. I hope you are excited about the future because God has a plan for you. Jeremiah 29:11 says: "'For I know the plans I have for you,' declares the Lord, 'plans to prosper you and not to harm you, plans to give you a hope and a future.'"

God wants you to get involved in his plan.

1. Plan to *be* the person that God says you can be.
2. Plan to *do* everything that God says you can do.
3. Plan to *receive* what God says you can receive.

"For everyone who asks receives; he who seeks finds; and to him who knocks, the door will be opened."
Matthew 7:8

When you depend on prayer, you will receive what God has planned for you. Jesus gave us a great example of prayer.

1. He began his ministry with prayer (Luke 3:21).
2. He prayed throughout the gospels. When the disciples saw him pray, they said, "Lord, teach us to pray" (Luke 11:1).
3. He prayed as he approached the cross (Luke 22:41-42).
4. He even prayed on the cross (Luke 23:43).

Think about it: How important is prayer in your personal life?

As a disciple, we need to begin each day with prayer.

1. God, I know you have a great day planned for me today.
2. I know you have the power to meet my spiritual, physical, emotional, and financial needs today.
3. Use me to bless the lives of other people today.
4. Help me fulfill your plan for my life today.

In Jesus name,
Amen

The Pattern Game on the next page teaches us some great principles about the future. Look at the game in illustration 9, give yourself one minute to begin with one and touch as many numbers in order as you can. Do this first before reading on.

We can probably help you touch more numbers if we give you some instructions. Look at the numbers by couplets like 1 and 2. The numbers have a pattern of go-

175

the pattern game

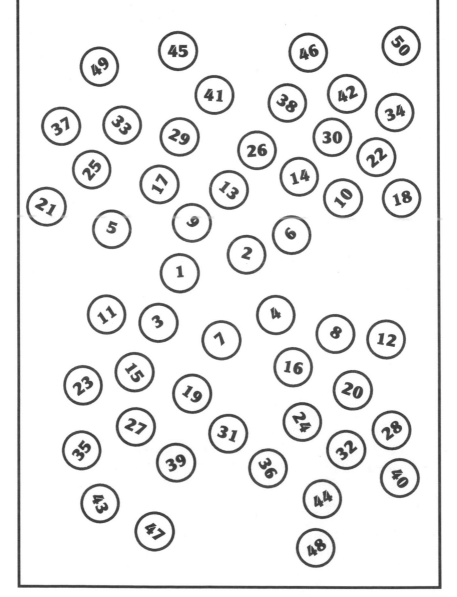

Illustration 9

ing from left to right in a zigzag by couplets. Look at the game and you will see how it works. Now, you should be able touch a lot more numbers in one minute because you know where you are going. Let's look at the church in the future and this should help us in the third millennium if we know where we are going.

Leadership

The leader for the new millennium needs to be a servant leader. He should work side by side in the trenches with the people. He needs to be seen as a fellow struggler. But, he should also be seen as a person of deep faith and prayer. He should have a passion to serve. He is a good listener and gathers input from the congregation before making decisions. He knows the values, mission, and vision of the congregation. There is a plan for the congregation . He strives to follow this plan and communicate the plan to the congregation. He doesn't control the church or manage the church. He equips others to use their gifts to fulfill the values, mission, and vision of the church.

> The leader for the new millennium should work side by side in the trenches with the people.

Ponder this: What kind of leader is needed for the new millennium?

He is more of a spiritual mentor than he is a board member. He is a tenderhearted shepherd interested in lost sheep. He cares about all the flock. He is good in dealing with change, conflict, and diversity. He helps others become spiritual giants.

He would rather delegate than do or control the task. He wants the church to be all that Jesus Christ wants it to be. He is interested in building teams of people who work together. He studies and networks so he can keep growing. He is much more interested in relationships with others than he is interested in authority. He trusts others and uses love of others for conformity and accountability.

He creates an environment for good change so the church can grow and prosper. He is not interested in teaching the facts to the head as much as he is interested in transforming the heart, and lives of the people. He is people-centered and offers spiritual guidance. His focus is on relationships and transforming lives more than religious knowledge and organization tasks. He encourages members to dream and start new ministries that implement the plan. It is evident the leader has a heart for God and longs to be in God's presence. He spends many hours in prayer and Bible study. He helps and encourages those involved in ministry. He pursues personal holiness. He knows what God wants him to do.

He leads his family spiritually. He demonstrates an active love for his neighborhood and performs acts of compassion for those in need. He is committed to close relationships for accountability. He demonstrates integrity and strives to have the mind of Christ. He delegates and empowers followers. He is aware of cultural trends and strives to use every available means to lead the different cultures to Jesus Christ. He understands what makes a healthy, growing church. He longs for the unity of God's people. He wants to produce dedicated disciples.

> Prayer is giving up my demands that others change and looking to God for the changes He sees I need.

Mentoring

The very best way to produce dedicated disciples is a process called mentoring. It was the plan that Jesus modeled for us. Almost 50% of the book of Mark is given to the time Jesus spent with his disciples. His leadership training plan looked something like this.

Jesus

Peter, James, John

Rest of the Apostles

Jesus' Leadership Training Plan

The needs of the world were tremendous during the time of Jesus. People everywhere were crying for his time. Yet, almost half his time was spent with this small leadership group. He knew what had to be done to produce disciples. There are no shortcuts. Church leaders need to be mentors of small groups for disciple training. This plan is also excellent for women's groups, youth groups and can be used intergenerationally. These regular meetings and activities will produce marvelous results.

Discuss:
How effective was Jesus' leadership training plan? How can it be translated to our modern society and work schedules?

The basic mentoring plan to follow is:

I do, you watch.

I do, you do with me.

You do, I watch.

You do, others watch.

Cycle repeats and both of us help someone else.

This kind of training produces competence, confidence, and spiritual success. The followers watch the mentor lead, teach, pray, study, and serve. They learn much from him. Then, the followers teach, pray, study, serve, and lead. The mentor watches and encourages them. He is also available to help them and offer advice. He is available when they need him. 70% of this plan is on-the-job training. The fourth step in the plan is where the followers now become men-

> The fourth step in the mentoring plan is where the followers now become mentors of others.

tors of others. It's the "you do, others watch" part. Thus Jesus' mentoring leadership training model had tremendous success as we look at it from the book of Acts.

Jesus
Mentor

Peter, James, John
Inner Circle

Other Apostles
Disciple Leaders

The 70
Support System

120 members
Base Congregation

3,000 to 5,000 members
The Converts

Growing And Declining Churches

Honestly ask:

Is your congregation a growing or a declining church?

The people of the 21st century will be most receptive to a church that is trying to transform lives to follow in the steps of Jesus. They are interested in following a map that will help them discover more and more about Jesus. They will see this as an incredible spiritual journey to the heart of God.

The Declining Church

1. The declining church of the future will be telling people how great their church is as they teach head facts with great knowledge. The lessons will not be tailor-made to connect with the needs of the people in the audience.
2. The declining church will spend much of their time on meetings and managing committees.
3. The declining church will have extreme difficulty making decisions.
4. The declining church will be training for membership.
5. The declining church will be serving only the church.
6. The declining church will be preoccupied with raising money.
7. The declining church pushes people to do church work.

The Growing Church

1. The growing church will be fulfilling their exciting mission as they go on a great spiritual journey.
2. The growing church will be doing hands-on ministry as well as training and equipping people for ministry.
3. The growing church will be pursuing their goal of making disciples.
4. The growing church will use praying members to serve.
5. The growing church will be serving the community.
6. The growing church will help people discover their gifts so they can be used for his glory. The growing church is preoccupied with rescuing people.
7. The growing church wants its members to find spiritual fulfillment.

180

8. The declining church retires from church work to let the younger set do it.
9. The declining church looks inward.
10. The declining church is eager to know everyone.

11. The declining church is loyal to tradition and one another.
12. The declining church is building faith on information.

13. The declining church has a major goal of perpetuating their past heritage.

8. The growing church pursues spiritual growth and Christian maturity in the spiritual race for life.
9. The growing church focuses outward.
10. The top priority for the growing church is for everybody to know God.
11. The growing church is trying to reach the unchurched.
12. The growing church is building faith on their experiences with prayer and Jesus Christ.
13. The growing church wants to follow the vision of Jesus Christ and his word for the future of the church. They are constantly asking: what would Jesus do? The growing church is interested in truly being the Church of Jesus Christ that he died for and purchased with his blood.

Bible School

The future of the Bible school needs to be a total adult education program developed much like the youth program. Sunday morning classes will center around friends and relationships. There will be much discussion and dialogue in classes as the Buster generation tends to tune out straight lecture in six to eight minutes. Multimedia presentations with PowerPoint can greatly increase attention span. Time is the most treasured commodity of the younger generation. They are accustomed to receiving information at a rapid pace in condensed form and then discussing it. For their curriculum, they are most interested in topics like:

1. How can I improve my marriage?
2. How can I manage my money better?
3. What can I do about my job that I don't like?

4. How do I get a better job?
5. How do I get out of addictive behavior and bad habits?
6. Where did the Bible come from? How do I know it is really God's word?
7. Why pray?
8. How can I be a better parent?
9. How can I make more time for myself?
10. How can I feel better about myself?

They are also interested in packaged studies from the Scriptures to deal with their major needs. Examples might be:

1. The Creation (Gen. 1–3) A look at God's power, plan, and provision for us. Also look at human beings' weaknesses and needs.
2. The 10 Commandments (Exod. 20:1-16) What God expects from me.
3. God's Purpose for My Life (Deut. 6:5)
4. What Really Matters on This Earth (Eccl. 12:13-14)
5. Why Jesus Came (Isa. 53)
6. The Basics of Christianity (Matt. 5–7)
7. How to Solve Disagreements (Matt. 18:15-18)
8. How to Be a Servant of Jesus (Matt. 20:20-28)
9. My Faith Should Be Shared (Matt. 28:19)
10. The Church in Action (Acts 2)
11. How to Love Someone You Can't Stand (Rom. 12:14-21)
12. The Importance of Submission (Romans 13:1-7)
13. Discovering and Using My Spiritual Gift (1 Cor. 12)
14. God's Plan for the Family (Eph. 5:22–6:4)
15. What Is Faith? (Heb. 11)
16. Holy Living for Dedicated Disciples (1 Thess. 5:15-22)

Prayer is accepting his gift of unchanging love.

The Sunday morning class should have many special projects which grow out of suggestions from the class. They will especially be interested in social issues such as providing for the poor or the widows. The class should strive to include every member.

There need to be many fellowship meetings because this group needs strong relationships. Family activities and recreational activities can be very beneficial.

Some consultants tell us there will be more people in Bible study Monday through Saturday than there will be on Sunday morning if we look ten years down the road. Many classes need to be scheduled throughout the week. This could include such courses as His Needs, Her Needs, Preparation for Marriage, How Families Can Grow in Prayer Together, Divorce Recovery, Financial Management, AA, and Grief Recovery. It will be more beneficial for us to take a weekly count of our Bible school attendance than just a count on Sunday morning. Individual records should be kept on each person in class so we can determine whom we are serving and how we are best meeting the needs of all our adults in the church and the community.

For you to consider: What benefit is there for the church in groups constituted to meet special needs? What are the drawbacks?

The ladies especially will want in-depth Bible classes for study and prayer with other ladies. These classes need to be scheduled throughout the week. Ladies will also enjoy week night services for women only. They speak, pray, lead singing, give testimonies, and share together. Men will also want some in-depth Bible studies throughout the week, but these will be a much smaller percentage. They also are more likely to prefer early morning instead of night.

The new generations have strong feelings and passions. They want to make a significant difference in today's world. They want to have a reason for studying what they are studying and doing what they are doing.

> The new generations want to have a reason for studying what they are studying and doing what they are doing. — a heart answer and not just a head answer.

183

They are more interested in a heart answer to this than a head answer. They want to feel good about their relationship with God, their families, friends, and other people. Their hearts can lead them to be evangelistic in the Adult Bible Class Program as they feel the need to share "their story" about why Jesus is important to them.

Small Groups

Small groups will become more important with each passing day. Younger generations like discussion and relationships. According to the Barna Report, small groups are composed of 68% women and 32% men. The peak ages to attend small groups are ages 28-46. Barna's research shows that geography has a lot to do with small groups. Only 12% of people in the Northeast and 19% in the West attended any small groups. On the other hand, 43% in the Midwest and 27% in the South attended small groups. His research also revealed a lot of ethnic differences in small groups. Sixty-nine percent of the attendees were white, 18% black, 7% Hispanics and 6% other.

Future small groups need to be very flexible and provide numerous options. The newer generations are longing for small groups with ice breakers to get better acquainted, sentence prayers where all pray, storytelling of how God is working in their life, singing, thanksgiving to God, appreciation for one another, Bible lessons and application and times of meditation.

> Small groups will become more important with each passing day.

To think about: What are the major purposes of your small groups? How well are they meeting their purposes?

Groups can be used for evangelism, discipling, equipping, shepherding, nurturing, Bible study involving to meet specific needs. Healthy groups multiply within three to six months. Some home church groups adhere to the following pattern:

First Hour — Some members arrive early to pray for God's power to work in the home church groups. Others arrive early for special prayers.

Second Hour — Fellowship and meal
Third Hour — Bible study and sharing.

It takes a lot of time to develop small groups and an accountability system. But they are an absolute necessity for future generations longing for relationships, shared feelings, and dialogue.

Stewardship

In the world of finance, most younger generations hate the words duty and commitment. They are so different from their parents in this area. Many Boomers and Busters are very cynical and feel that all the church wants is money. Therefore, we must have an honest, up-front approach with them so they can grow to be dedicated disciples who tithe. We must address these major areas with them:

> Many feel that all the church wants is money.

Ponder this question: What are some of the causes of cynicism in regard to the church and money?

1. We must help them be better managers of money when they ask us to.
2. We must provide money management classes to meet their needs. Most of them are overwhelmed with consumer debt.
3. We must emphasize the needs of people in our giving and not buildings. If we must build new facilities for children, call it something like "our children's building."
4. They are not nearly as interested in paying off debt as they are in meeting the needs of people.
5. Boomers and busters are interested in giving to projects which will help them and their families.
6. Teaching on giving in small groups or small Bible classes is much more effective with them than auditorium sermons.
7. They are reached through their hearts first and then their heads. Testimonies in class of people who have been helped give them a passion to serve.
8. They will more readily give to a tragedy involving people in a region than they will to missions.

9. Giving to missions must utilize personal stories of transformed lives in the mission area.
10. Dialogue is necessary for them in the giving groups and classes. They need to experience the feelings and passions of those who have given to certain causes.
11. Their giving will originally be motivated by the feelings, examples, and passions of their friends instead of an in-depth message on giving.
12. They will watch videotapes filled with the importance of meeting the needs of people.
13. They will respond to prayer guides about praying for the needs of people.
14. They are more interested in meeting the needs of the people than a budget they do not understand.
15. They are more interested in producing disciples than making decisions about giving.
16. They will give with passion to whatever transforms lives.
17. They will follow the giving example of leaders in their peer group.
18. The more hands-on involvement they have in a ministry, the greater their giving.

> Love their children and their money will follow.

19. They need to see giving as a joy and not a burden.
20. They need to feel good about the Values, Mission, and Vision statements of the church.
21. Be very patient with them. Show them your love.
22. Love their children and their money will follow.
23. Offer multiple options for them to give to certain areas where they have greater interest.
24. Shower them with gratitude for their giving. Mail them a thank you note two to four times a year.
25. Let them know what's in it for them personally.
26. Now that you have captured their hearts, you can teach their heads the spiritual nature of giving.

27. Teach them to set priorities and win the battle over materialism.
28. Share with them the passion God has to share everything with them.
29. Teach them God made us and wants us to give back to him what he has loaned to us as stewards.
30. Teach them that dedicated disciples have discovered the joy in the statement: "It is more blessed to give than to receive."
31. Teach them the importance of giving 10%. Have people in their age bracket share testimonies about this.
32. Teach them not to give because of coercion, but to give out of their gratitude to God.
33. Have them pray and discuss how they can become tithers. Open, nonjudgmental dialogue are imperative with this group.
34. Have them discuss Matthew 22:37-40.
35. Have them discuss why one-sixth of the words of Jesus and two-thirds of his parables are about money.
36. Leaders should personally pray for members by name to be on a journey to become dedicated disciples who are spiritual tithers.

Women's Role

The women's role in the church continues to expand. Since two out of every three visitors at church are women, they need to see other women being used for the glory of God. It's women who are bringing their families to church for the first time. It's women who are leading the way. I pray that men will long to be spiritual leaders in their families — but this isn't happening much among the unchurched. When these women arrive at services, they should see husband and wife teams at the door as greeters. They should have

> Prayer is praising God through my tears when my day is at its darkest.

For your consideration: How important are female role models to the growth of the church?

187

women counselors made available to help them with their problems. Women who have been sexually abused are not likely to respond to a man. Women can lead great women's ministries. They will be coordinating nursery and children's classes. Many will be trained to work with teenage girls in youth programs. They will take care of most of the food and fellowship. They provide tremendous leadership in the church through their secretarial roles. They will be active in singing groups and prayer ministry. Most of our teachers in Bible school are women. Women in the future will likely be leaders in our counseling programs and benevolent ministries. They have a tremendous passion to serve. They will also continue to develop prayer ministries and prayer rooms. They will be the ones who continue to teach most of their children to pray. Thank God for women who serve. I don't know what we would do without you. Tomorrow's generation is not as interested in the traditional role of women in the church. May God help all of us empty our cups, fill us with his spirit, and help all of us discover the biblical role of women from his word.

> Prayer is realizing that God is the God of TODAY carrying out his purposes in every boring, lonely minute of my life.

Evaluation time:
What do you personally like or dislike about how your worship service is set up right now? What comments have you heard from others?

Worship

The major goal of worship for future generations will be to provide an experience to transform lives. It will try to connect with people where they are and lead them to be all God wants them to be. If you have several generations represented in your congregation in large numbers, you may want to have several different kinds of services. No service is better than any other service — but we must connect to future generations. I devoted one chapter to worship in *The Servant-Driven Church*, and you may want to refer to it for reference. The most difficult thing to do is to meet the needs and desires of members as well as reach the unchurched. This section will deal primarily with reaching the millions of Boomers and Busters who are unchurched.

Future worship services for this group need to be very visual. They learn by sight and sound. We need to create a visual experience for them. Screens, video, drama, PowerPoint, Scriptures and pictures on screen, and outlines will all be very important to them.

They also like loud sound that surrounds them. They like all the feelings, passion, and emotions this creates. The service needs to be supported with the latest technology.

Services will also be more personal and spontaneous. There will be more stories told from the Bible and more testimonies. Services will tend to be more open ended to encourage people to think and express feelings.

Services will be much more participatory. The preacher may call out a question like: "Who did you come here to worship?" The audience would call out together with one accord: "Jesus!"

This generation will be reached first through the heart and then through the head. They need to experience a church that cares about people and their needs.

Most of the announcements need to be on the screen. Generation-X watch TV commercials as much as they watch programs!

Future generations will tend to not want fixed pews. They will tend to want tables and chairs in a large space setting. The service will be very relaxed. These people are looking for a place to call home and a haven for rest. They want a message that addresses today's needs in a pragmatic way. The message needs to stress grace and acceptance more than sin.

These generations want to express praise and gratitude to God. The service will be done in the culture of

Discuss with others:

What do you consider the main goal or purpose of corporate worship? How well is that purpose being met in your congregation?

> Generation-X watch TV commercials as much as they watch programs!

today, and this is called Indigenous Worship. These people are on a journey searching for an authentic Christian community. They are looking for honesty and integrity. Many options need to be offered to them because they are multisensory and learn through all eight intelligences. They are more interested in people than principles. They are more interested in attitudes than different ages.

Generation-X is looking for a caring Christ, and they are looking for survival instead of a big cause. They are looking for a life raft to rescue them.

Boomers want to exalt Christ. They believe God is unfolding history, and they are looking for a cause. They want a highly choreographed service.

All of the groups are looking for a road map to follow. They are looking for fellow strugglers who will walk this walk with them.

They especially like stories and relate to prayers. They believe strongly in prayer, and it builds a bridge to all generations.

The single biggest thing that keeps us from connecting with the unchurched is our music. They like to hear familiar contemporary music that is currently on the radio and television. They do not know or relate to most of the older Christian hymns. They like to sing directly to God instead of about him.

> All of the groups are looking for a road map to follow.

Christian Copyright Licensing International (on the Web at www.ccli.com) keeps track of the songs being used in churches in order to award royalties to the copyright owners. Here is the list of the top 25 worship songs for the period April 1, 1998, to September 30, 1998. (The number in parentheses is the ranking of that song in the top 10 for 1995.)

1. *Lord, I Lift Your Name on High*, by Rick Founds (5)
2. *As the Deer,* by Marty Neystrom (6)
3. *He Has Made Me Glad,* by Leona Van Brethorst (4)
4. *I Love You, Lord,* by Laurie Klein (2)

5. *Majesty,* by Jack Hayford (3)
6. *Give Thanks,* by Henry Smith (1)
7. *Awesome God,* by Rich Mullins
8. *Shout to the Lord,* by Darlene Zschech
9. *He Is Exalted,* by Twila Paris
10. *Glorify Thy Name,* by Donna Akins (8)
11. *We Bring the Sacrifice,* by Kirt Dearman (7)
12. *All Hail, King Jesus,* by Dave Moody (9)
13. *Change My Heart, Oh God,* by Eddie Espinosa
14. *This Is the Day,* by Les Garrett
15. *More Precious Than Silver,* by Lynn DeShazo
16. *I Will Call upon the Lord,* by Michael O'Shields
17. *Lord, the Light of Your Love,* by Graham Kendrick
18. *I Exalt Thee,* by Pete Sanchez, Jr.
19. *How Majestic Is Your Name,* by Michael W. Smith
20. *Great Is the Lord,* by Michael W. & Deborah E. Smith
21. *Open Our Eyes,* by Bob Cull
22. *Holy Ground,* by Geron Davis
23. *Celebrate Jesus,* by Gary Oliver
24. *Jesus, Name above All Names,* by Naida Hearn (10)
25. *Because He Lives,* by William J. & Gloria Gaither

Try this: List your own favorite songs. Ask your parents (or someone else of that generation) to list theirs. Do the same with your children.

Some of you are saying: "I love the old hymns. They are more spiritual than the new songs." Most of the older songs were written by church leaders hundreds of years ago. Most of the new songs come straight out of the word of God! I don't think the issue is words as much as it is the music. Where did the music sic from the older hymns come from? Many of them came out of beer taverns. These church **Prayer** leaders who wrote the songs wanted to **is** connect with the unchurched of **accepting** their day so they used the music **God's GRACE.** sung in the beer taverns. I have a German stein with a music box. You wind it up and you hear the music to the great hymn we sing at baptisms "O Happy Day." It was originally the music to a beer song called "Come Drink With Me!"

191

Generation-X loves rap and songs that repeat over and over. I have a taped recording that demonstrates some of the chants in the early church. It sounds like a slow rap, and most of us don't like it. I think we need to get on our knees and pray for God's forgiveness and wisdom. It's ridiculous for us to be arguing about some of these things when we know the whole story. Let's pray for a church in the third millennium that reaches the unchurched with the gospel of Christ.

Closing Remarks

We've talked a lot in this last chapter about the future of the church. Nobody but God knows for sure what will happen. I'm certainly not saying all these trends are good or bad. Some of them are very difficult for me to deal with. But based upon hundreds of hours of study and research, these are the trends I see for the future. We must reach these younger generations with the gospel of Christ. I also know that prayer will get the church ready for the future. There are four things that | Prayer will get the church ready for the future. | will continue in the future.

Answer this honestly: How well do you handle criticism?

1. Criticism — You will be criticized in the future. If it's good criticism that is justified, respond to it and change. If it is unjustified criticism that only wants to tear you and the church down, remember that you can't "outpuke a buzzard." Don't deal with this group of people if it won't do any good. As when Nehemiah was building the wall, keep your eyes on Jesus and don't respond to unjust criticism.

2. Grace — Church and unchurched need to hear a message of grace in the third millennium more than ever before. Let me share a story to stress this important point:

Several years ago I was asked to speak at the San Antonio Convention Center. I arrived at the La Quinta Motel at 5:00 p.m. and was supposed to speak at 7:00 p.m. I went immediately to the swimming pool for a short swim. I slipped a styrofoam life preserver around my midsection to float around for a while. At 5:30 p.m., I got out of the pool and made a startling discovery. Styrofoam expands when it gets wet, and I could not get it from around my midsection. I went to the shower in my motel room with the life preserver around me. I tried shampoo, lotion and all the strength I had to get rid of the life preserver. It was a hopeless cause. It's now 6:00 p.m. I slowly walk over **We cannot be saved without God's grace.** to the motel office and open the door. I said: "I've got a problem." The lady responded, " I see you've got a problem" and died laughing. I asked if there was any way she could help me. She said, "Yes, there's a butcher knife back in the kitchen. That scared me, and I really tried to get the life preserver off of me now. I tried as hard as I could, and I have never sweat so much in my life — but I could not get the life preserver off. She finally came back with the butcher knife. She sawed the life preserver off of me and didn't cut me too badly. I walked on the stage to speak at two minutes to 7:00 p.m.

It taught me a great lesson. No matter how hard I worked, I couldn't get that life preserver off. We cannot work our way to heaven. We cannot be saved without God's grace.

3. Forgiveness and Prayer — The Bible teaches us to confess our sins to one another and pray for each other (Jas. 5:16). The church would be so much better off if we followed this principle in the third millennium. I was preaching once at the Fifth Ward Church of Christ in Houston, and a beautiful girl came forward. I was a little nervous. She said: "I want to confess my sins. I need the prayers of this church because I have been having an affair." Then, she pointed her finger at a man in the audience and said: "I've

Some more self-evaluation: How hard is it for you to accept forgiveness or for you to forgive someone else?

Final question:
What are great
bridge builders
for the future
of the church?
Can you expand
on the statement
made here?

been having an affair with that man, and he also needs to confess his sins!" And he did!

Forgiveness and prayer will be great bridge builders for the future of the church.

The 23rd Psalm
For the Prayer-Driven Church

The Lord is our shepherd, His church shall not want.
He makes His church pause for prayer.
He leads His church by the power of prayer.
He restores His church.
He leads us in the paths of righteousness for His church's sake.
Yea, though we walk through the valley of difficult times,
We will fear no evil; For He is with His church.
The Bible and prayers answered comfort us.
We feel his presence at communion on the first day of the week.
When we remember, pray, fellowship, celebrate, and forgive,
He anoints His church with the power of the Holy Spirit;
Our blessings overflow.
Surely goodness and mercy shall follow His church
All the days of our life,
And we will dwell in the House of Prayer forever!

Ray Fulenwider

Other Recommended Books for Study

Anderson, Dr. Lynn. *They Smell Like Sheep*. West Monroe, LA: Howard Publishing, 1997,

Armour, Dr. Michael and Don Browning. *Systems—Sensitive Leadership*. Joplin, MO: College Press, 1995.

Barna, George. *The Second Coming of the Church*. Nashville: Word Publishing, 1998.

Bisagno, John. *The Power of Positive Praying*. Grand Rapids: Zondervan, 1965.

Bounds, E.M. *The Complete Works of E.M. Bounds on Prayer*. Grand Rapids: Baker Books, 1990.

Carbonell, Dr. Mels. *Uniquely You*. Blue Ridge, GA: Leadership Institute of America, 1998.

Christenson, Evelyn. *What Happens When Women Pray*. Wheaton, IL: Victor Books, 1979.

Easum, William. *Sacred Cows Make Gourmet Burgers*. Nashville: Abingdon Press, 1995.

_____. *Strategic Strategies for Change, Transformational Leadership, Disciples Making Leaders, Worship, Growing Spiritual Redwoods, Life Changing Small Group Ministry*. Port Aransas, TX: 21st Century Strategies, 1998.

Ellas, Dr. John. *Measuring Church Growth*. Houston: Center for Church Growth, 1997.

Ferguson, Dr. Everett. *The Church of Christ*. Grand Rapids: Eerdmans, 1996.

_____. *Early Christians Speak*. Austin: Sweet Publishing, 1971.

_____. *The New Testament Church*. Abilene, TX: Abilene Christian University Press, 1990.

Fulenwider, Ray. *The Servant-Driven Church*. Joplin, MO: College Press, 1997.

Hanks, Louis. *Vision, Variety and Vitality*. Nashville: Convention Press, 1996.

Haugh, Kenneth C. *Reopening the Back Door: Answers to Questions about Ministering to Inactive Members*. Tebunah Ministries, 1992.

Hodge, Charles. *Prayer, the Voice of Faith*. Searcy, AR: Resource Publications, 1996.

Houts, Keneth. *You Are a Miracle Waiting to Happen*. Shippensburg: Destiny Image Publishers, 1996.

Jones, Laurie Beth. *JESUS CEO: Using Ancient Wisdom for Visionary Leadership*. New York: Hyperion, 1995.

Kagan, Dr. Spencer and Miguel. *Multiple Intelligences*. San Clemente, CA: Kagan Cooperative Learning, 1998.

Latourette, Dr. Kenneth. *A History of Christianity*. Vol. 1 and 2. New York: Harper and Row, 1975.

Malphurs, Aubrey. *Values Driven Leadership*. Grand Rapids: Baker, 1995.

Maxwell, Dr. John. *Partners in Prayer*. Nashville: Thomas Nelson Publishing, 1996.

McGlothlin, Dr. W.J. *A Guide to the Study of Church History*. Louisville: Baptist World Publishing, 1908.

Murren, Doug. *The Baby Boomerang*. Ventura, CA: Regal Books, 1990.

Omartian, Stormie. *The Power of a Praying Wife*. Eugene, OR: Harvest House, 1997.

Panati, Charles. *Sacred Origins of Profound Things*. New York: Penguin Group, 1996.

Rinker, Rosalind. *Prayer: Conversing with God*. Grand Rapids: Zondervan, 1965.

Sanders, J. Oswald. *Prayer Power Unlimited*. Chicago: Moody Press, 1977.

Torrey, Dr. R.A. *How to Pray*. Minneapolis: Whitaker House, 1983.

Walker, Dr. Williston. *A History of the Christian Church*. New York: Charles Scribners Sons, 1943.

Water, Mark. *Prayer Made Easy*. Peabody, MA: Hendrickson Publishers, 1999.

Ray Fulenwider has done it again. His Gold Medallion nominee book *The Servant-Driven Church* was a huge blessing to the kingdom. *The Prayer-Driven Church* will surely even surpass that. These are great days to develop great teams of great prayer warriors — ro receive great blessings from our great God.

Lynn Anderson
President of Hope Network Ministries
Dallas, Texas

Once again Ray has hit a home run. It's helpful to receive these practical truths and new concepts from the "trenches" rather than the "Ivory Towers." The genius is that through this base of need we are drawn to the Power Source.

Dr. Gary R. Beauchamp
Senior Minister, Highland Oaks Church of Christ
Dallas, Texas

I have climbed the physical peaks and mountains of the world experiencing combat on three continents and sailing on all major oceans: I acknowledge the value of an experienced and skilled guide to stay alive.

Ray Fulenwider is that type of guide who inspires spiritual confidence to lift you through life's obstacles and then to guide you through the working stages of *The Servant-Driven Church*, Ray's excellent preceding book.

In this new book *The Prayer-Driven Church* Ray skillfully guides and directs both experienced and new Christians on how to avoid a disaster in the making and how to become involved in structuring a truly mission-minded church through PRAYER.

The Prayer-Driven Church is a living example of the stark beauty of a bright star in a dark sky. Ray's spiritual insight brings into focus the awesome reality that prayer is the single greatest responsibility and privilege for a church to have which leads it to be known as a "Church of Prayer."

The Prayer-Driven Church is a powerful foundation document as a main study guide for building a prayer-driven church.

Billy R. Duncan
Colonel of Marines, Retired
Director, CIS Foundation
Elder, Paramount Terrace Christian Church
Amarillo, Texas

Place all your church planning on hold! *The Prayer-Driven Church* provides the place to begin and reveals the true source of all growth. Ray Fulenwider presents much more than concepts and theory. Here are practical and usable insights based on decades of experience that God has richly blessed.

Let me speak plainly. Most congregations believe they are praying churches when in reality they're not. There is no greater nor more important concern than the need to develop praying churches. Ray Fulenwider's book, *The Prayer-Driven Church*, is a timely gift and labor of love. I highly recommend that leaders study it, implement the practical strategies, and become a house of prayer.

Dr. John W. Ellas
Director, Center for Church Growth
Houston, Texas

Don't eat! Don't shower! Don't go out!!!
Don't do anything else until you've read Ray's book — *The Prayer-Driven Church.*
The best part is — RAY LIVES IT!
Story after story — success after success — Ray shows us a God who is eager to embrace our prayers — AND EAGER TO ANSWER THEM!
Better do it NOW (before you get to heaven) — else the Lord will say. "What?! You had a chance to read Ray's book — and practice the POWER OF PRAYER — and you did not do it?!

Dr. Neil Gallagher
Dallas, Texas
Radio and television show host
Author of 25 books on Christian morality and ethics
Elder, minister, Financial advisor and consultant

I've known Ray Fulenwider for the last 30 years and seen God do incredible things through him as great churches were built at Broadway in Lubbock, Richland Hills in Ft. Worth and Central in Amarillo. But by far the greatest work he has ever done is writing *The Prayer-Driven Church*!

Bill Johnson
Elder at Central Church of Christ
Amarillo, Texas

I believe Ray's book, *The Prayer-Driven Church,* is right on target for the next millennium. I especially enjoyed the personal stories and examples. Ray is a great servant.

Dick Marcear
Senior Minister, Central Church of Christ
Amarillo, Texas

The Prayer-Driven Church will help Christians get in touch with God's prayer power. It's a must read book for those who are looking for a new, Bible-based paradigm for churches to follow in the new millennium.

Dr. John C. Maxwell
Founder, The INJOY Group
Norcross, Georgia

I have had the distinct blessing of being able to read the manuscript of Ray Fulenwider's new book entitled *The Prayer-Driven Church.* The faith, prayer and Christlike zeal for the lost set forth in this book will motivate congregations to grow much like those of the first century. Especially enjoyable are the various programs described where almost every member can participate but where the Heavenly Father receives the glory and honor.

Jule L. Miller
Gospel Services
Houston, Texas
Producer of filmstrips and videos that have
been responsible for over 50,000 conversions

[The Prayer-Driven Church] is practical and down-to-earth and will no doubt inspire many Christians to a deeper life of prayer. [Ray] certainly has his priorities right — prayer comes first. There are many good words from the Word about prayer. That's always in order.

Dr. Royce Money
President, Abilene Christian University
Abilene, Texas

There is one word for *The Prayer-Driven Church:* WOW! Two words: "GET IT!" Three words: "THANK YOU, RAY!" Four words: "YOU WILL BE BLESSED!"

The Prayer-Driven Church (PDC) follows on the heels of Rick Warren's *The Purpose-Driven Church,* and Ray Fulenwider's earlier work, *The Servant-Driven Church.* They are a trilogy; you need all three.

PDC takes us on a twelve-chapter, "base-path journey" from praying members to active evangelists to involved servants to dedicated disciples. Chapter One, "The Power of Prayer," ought to be read by every eldership in the church. One whole chapter deals with the power God bestows when women pray. We often make feeble attempts at evangelism without much success. Ray uses one whole chapter showing that prayer is the foundation for evangelism.

There are four books I recommend to our leaders today for real, biblical church growth. Rick Warren's *The Purpose-Driven Church,* Jim Cymbalas' *Fresh Wind, Fresh Fire*; Ray has powerfully written the other two: *The Servant-Driven Church* and this one, *The Prayer-Driven Church.* Get them. Read and digest them. Use the powerful, biblical ideas he outlines. Allow your church to enjoy the fruits of God-approved growth!

Marvin Phillips
Marvin Phillips Ministries
Tulsa, Oklahoma

The Prayer-Driven Church is one more enthusiastic move by Ray Fulenwider to spur us on to greater effectiveness. Prayer causes church to be done right. Ray has been there . . . and done that.

Terry Rush
Memorial Drive Church of Christ
Tulsa, Oklahoma

If we are serious about restoring the life and ministry of the first-century church in our own time and place, we must learn the significance of prayer. We must teach the importance of prayer. We must build our churches and ministries around prayer. But we must do more than study, teach, and build ministries around it. *We must pray and pray and pray.* Ray Fulenwider has served us again by calling us to be people and churches who define our existence on our knees.

Dr. Rubel Shelly
Senior Minister, Woodmont Hills Church of Christ
Nashville, Tennessee

The Prayer-Driven Church is spiritual dynamite for church leaders. It should be required reading for every leader.

Myron Stewart
Elder
Houston, Texas

In *The Prayer-Driven Church* Ray calls us to claim the power which God promises us when we pray. He says, "If there is any one message I want to emphasize for the third millennium, it is the power God provides when we pray." What could the church need more? What could be more helpful to each of us individually? But the book not only emphasizes the needs, it gives practical guidelines for becoming a prayer-driven church. He cites ways a congregation can emphasize prayer, with numerous examples.

One chapter is entitled, "What Happens When Women Pray?" emphasizing the major role women play in teaching children to pray, in praying for unchristian husbands and other relatives, as well as praying for other church concerns and the needs of the world.

The main emphasis of the Bible-based book is to help all of us get in touch with God's prayer power. It will be a blessing to the leadership of a congregation as they seek the spiritual growth of the church. It can be used in a small group study, or it can be a help to us individually as we seek to become more prayer-driven.

I encourage you to read this book for your own growth in prayer, but also to share with your congregation an emphasis on prayer that will make your church a prayer-driven church.

Helen M. Young
Malibu, California

About the Author

Ray Fulenwider is the new Minister of Administration and Church Coordination for the Spring Woodlands Church of Christ in Houston, Texas, as of February 1, 2000. This 1100 member congregation plans major expansion for the next 10 years. The address is:

Spring Woodlands Church of Christ   Phone: 281-367-2304
1021 Sawdust Road   email: ray@swcc.net
Spring, Texas 77380-2151   Fax: 281-367-9995

From 1991 to 2000 Ray Fulenwider has served as the Minister of Education and Involvement, Staff Coordinator and Office Manager at Central Church of Christ in Amarillo, Texas. Central was  really struggling in 1991 when Ray arrived, but today the vibrant congregation is the home of 2500 men, women, boys, and girls. Ray earned his BSE and MSE degrees from Abilene Christian University and has done grad- uate studies in New York, Tennessee and Texas. He re- ceived an Administration de- gree and counselors license from Texas Tech.

Ray began preaching at the age of twelve and has held ministries in churches of all sizes. In addition, he has worked in all types of jobs from pulling and chopping cotton to teaching at the uni- versity level (Pepperdine Uni- versity, Oklahoma Christian University, Harding Univer- sity, Lubbock Christian College, Abilene Christian University, The University of Texas and David Lipscomb University). He has been a principal and coach in the Texas pub- lic school system. He has directed workshops for Bible school teachers. For 25 years he was the coordinator for Church Growth and Involvement Seminars held semi-annually. These seminars have attracted over 12,000 people from 40 states and 5 foreign coun- tries. He has also hosted a weekly cable television program entitled "Coping" and served as president of the American Cancer Society as well as being Executive Director of the Richland Hills Counseling Center and serving on the executive board of Texas Alcohol Narcotics Education.

When it comes to church growth, Ray speaks from experience. From 1968-1978 with the Broadway Church of Christ in Lubbock, Texas, and from 1978-1990 with the Richland Hills Church of Christ, he helped attendance in all services (already at the sev- eral hundred level) to double and even triple.

Ray has spoken throughout the United States and in two foreign countries. He has conducted over 350 leadership retreats for elders and deacons. He has written *Servant- Driven Church* and *How to Grow a Church through the Bible School* and has edited Bible school curricula and the magazines *Gospel Advocate* and *20th Century Christian*. He has also been a contributing editor to *Image Magazine*.

Ray is married to Ann and together they have four children: Deana, Jeana, Joel, and Jana. Ann has taught preschool and children's Bible classes for over 25 years.